BODY
OF
PROOF

"'I am the resurrection and the life.' These words of Jesus in the Gospel of John show that resurrection is not ancillary to Christian faith, nor an optional extra that can be selected or omitted. In this insightful book, Jeremiah Johnston demonstrates both why resurrection remains core to authentic Christian faith and why it's reasonable to believe in the bodily resurrection of Jesus. He marshals evidence and arguments that some readers may not have previously encountered. In the process, he carefully explains not only the centrality of resurrection faith for Christianity, but also provides a more solid basis for the reasoned support of such a faith. Johnston has done a great service both for those who hold to the Christian faith and for those who are open enquirers seeking to assess the merits of the truth claims of Christianity for themselves. All who read this book will be stimulated to ask deeper questions and to answer them in a more compelling manner."

Paul Foster, professor of New Testament and early Christianity
School of Divinity, University of Edinburgh

"With arguments both traditional and new—appealing to recent evidence concerning Jesus' tomb and considerations of second-century challenges concerning the resurrection story—Johnston both persuades and encourages us. He demonstrates that Jesus' resurrection makes sense of life and is the centerpiece of our hope."

Craig S. Keener, F. M. and Ada Thompson Professor
of biblical studies, Asbury Theological Seminary

"Dr. Jeremiah Johnston is on the front lines of battle, ensuring a biblical worldview is clear and present as students, staff, teachers, and parents gear up to defend the Christian faith. *Body of Proof* is a strong injection of truth around the foundational principle of the resurrection of Christ. This truth strengthens our faith and fortifies our relationship with the One who died in our place and rose again with the Ultimate Victory!"

Michael Goddard, EdD, superintendent
of Prestonwood Christian Academy

"In this very important book, renowned New Testament scholar and my dear personal friend Dr. Jeremiah Johnston provides us with seven compelling reasons to believe in the resurrection of Jesus Christ. In a world and culture where many are struggling to know what they believe and why, the profound truths in this book will shore up your faith and set your heart on fire."

Sheila Walsh, bestselling author and television host

"Here's a creative masterpiece of persuasive evidence for the pivotal event of human history—the resurrection of Jesus. Dr. Johnston's unique and thoroughly researched approach is sure to solidify the faith of Christians and challenge the skepticism of doubters. Historical facts for the resurrection are what brought me from atheism to faith many years ago—and perhaps this lively and convicting work will transform your life as well. Read it with a highlighter handy!"

Lee Strobel, *New York Times* bestselling author, and founding director of the Lee Strobel Center at Colorado Christian University

"*Body of Proof* is an important book because the resurrection of Jesus is the most important event in human history. Dr. Jeremiah Johnston knows the relevant scholarship, and he knows how to present it in a readable, persuasive way. Highly recommended."

Craig A. Evans, John Bisagno Distinguished Professor of Christian Origins, Houston Christian University

"In every generation, new challenges and piercing questions arise in a culture constantly drifting away from God. Thankfully, the truth never changes. Our faith is anchored in the historical fact of Jesus' physical resurrection. However, after pastoring for decades, I am burdened by the fact many believers are themselves ill-equipped to defend the truth of Jesus' resurrection and indifferent to the transformation of a resurrection-centric life. Our own pastor of apologetics and cultural engagement, Dr. Jeremiah J. Johnston, studied and defended the resurrection of Jesus at the highest intellectual levels, but with the heart of a pastor, he distills the best evidence for Jesus' resurrection. *Body of Proof* is a book every pastor should teach and every believer read, because in enhancing our own understanding of the resurrection, we solidify the faith once and for all delivered. I'm honored to be Jeremiah's pastor and friend and have a front-row seat to his relentless love for Christ and His unchanging Word. I heartily recommend *Body of Proof*."

Dr. Jack Graham, Senior Pastor of Prestonwood Baptist Church

BODY
OF
PROOF

THE **7** BEST REASONS TO BELIEVE
IN THE RESURRECTION OF JESUS—
AND WHY IT MATTERS TODAY

JEREMIAH J. JOHNSTON, PhD

BETHANYHOUSE
a division of Baker Publishing Group
Minneapolis, Minnesota

Published by Bethany House Publishers
Minneapolis, Minnesota
www.bethanyhouse.com

Bethany House Publishers is a division of
Baker Publishing Group, Grand Rapids, Michigan

Printed in the United States of America

Library of Congress Cataloging-in-Publication Data
Names: Johnston, Jeremiah, author.
Title: Body of proof : the 7 best reasons to believe in the resurrection of Jesus-and why it matters today / Jeremiah J. Johnston, PhD.
Description: Minneapolis, Minnesota : Bethany House Publishers, a division of Baker Publishing Group, 2023. | Includes bibliographical references. | Summary: "Straightforward and practical, Body of Proof examines the latest archaeological and textual findings and presents seven tangible, fresh proofs that Jesus really rose from the dead-and why it matters Today. When you fully understand the implications of the resurrection, you will begin to understand the power of Christ in you. And it changes everything"–Provided by publisher.
Identifiers: LCCN 2022049811 | ISBN 9780764230837 (paperback) | ISBN 9780764242410 (casebound) | ISBN 9781493440726 (ebook)
Subjects: LCSH: Jesus Christ—Resurrection—Biblical teaching.
Classification: LCC BT482 .J66 2023 | DDC 232/.5—dc23/eng/20230224
LC record available at https://lccn.loc.gov/2022049811

Cover design by LOOK Design Studio

Author is represented by Law Office of Curtis W. Wallace, P.C.

Baker Publishing Group publications use paper produced from sustainable forestry practices and post-consumer waste whenever possible.

24 25 26 27 28 29   8 7 6 5 4

For Justin,
my best friend and firstborn son

In the earliest days of Christianity an "apostle" was first and foremost a man who claimed to be an eyewitness of the Resurrection . . . to preach Christianity meant primarily to preach the Resurrection.

—C. S. Lewis, *Miracles*

Contents

Contents

Foreword

As Dr. Jeremiah Johnston notes at the outset of this book, too seldom are there series of sermons or Bible studies on the resurrection of Jesus. Yet this event is unquestionably at the very center of the New Testament proclamation. Paul stated that, apart from this event, the very faith of his hearers was vain and they were still in their sins (1 Corinthians 15:17). How often do believers today hear words such as these?

The subject of Jesus' resurrection occupies more than three hundred verses in the canonical New Testament. These texts typically describe either the historical testimony and facticity of this event or its being the very center of the gospel message of the deity, death, and resurrection of Jesus. But while the gospel teaching and the apologetic significance of this message are probably the most common applications of this occurrence, the resurrection is connected to almost every major theological doctrine as well as many, if not most, areas of the practical application and practice of the Christian faith. The plethora of New Testament texts combine the truth and importance of the resurrection with each of these additional topics, spotlighting the attention it receives throughout.

Dr. Johnston sets forth seven key reasons for the truth of Jesus' resurrection, which contain both factual as well as practical applications. The initial point includes multiple areas of world transformation wherever the gospel message is embraced—that the Son of God died for the sins of the world and rose again, introducing the possibility of freedom and social change. Next, these historical events were dated in space and time, where on the third day after Jesus' crucifixion, death was transformed into victory. Further, Jesus demonstrated his resurrection power in that, while others were reportedly raised to die again, Jesus was raised immortally.

Perhaps surprising to some, the Jews did not conceive of individuals rising bodily and immortally before the end of time, hence there was no reason to invent the resurrection event. Moreover, the available written and archaeological sources indicate the truth of both the empty tomb and Jesus' post-resurrection appearances, including eyewitness testimony to the latter. Additionally, the conversions of those who were not previously Jesus' followers, such as the transformation of Paul, changed the world. Last, that believers can share the results of the resurrection serves as the only ultimate answer to the problem of suffering. Believers are actually invited to live immortally as well!

Body of Proof closes with discussions of two final considerations. Dr. Johnston refers to these as "the new frontier." First, the more likely of the two most popular supposed physical locations of Jesus' empty burial tomb is discussed in detail. And last, the observation is made and defended that if the early church invented the resurrection story, they did a terrible job of it!

All told, this text moves along promptly in setting forth a variety of both historical information as well as applicable lessons. In other words, Dr. Johnston realizes that a solid case for the resurrection involves both head and heart working together. Not only did this message throughout the New Testament move into the deeper waters of careful testimonies of quite real resurrection appearances, but the exceptionally early proclamation of this message transformed lives. Further, the proclamation spread to the areas that reach human hearts, such as the preaching of the gospel, the transformation of the world, and there being a truly sustainable answer to the pithiest problem of human existence by offering life forever.

This is a huge task, and Dr. Johnston needs to be given credit for jumping in with both feet and in the process showing the reader how all these various tasks can be combined in order to bring about a truly beautiful, fully orbed answer to the ongoing quest for truth, meaning, beauty, and peace—even for eternity!

Gary R. Habermas, PhD
Distinguished Research Professor
Liberty University

Introduction

The twentieth-century German literary giant and novelist Franz Kafka was fond of saying, "The meaning of life is that it ends," and for most the end comes all too soon. But then what happens? "If a man dies, shall he live again?" (Job 14:14) is a deeply theological and practical question pondered in the earliest writings of the Old Testament. How we come to answer this question of life after death is a game changer.

Unfortunately, far too many Christians are clumsy about their resurrection faith. While numerically stagnate, a majority of American Christians may profess belief in resurrection, but far fewer can, in the cultural vernacular, confidently share the reasons they're confident Jesus rose from the dead. You can test this by asking friends in your next Bible study group meeting to offer more than a *Because the Bible told me so* answer for the evidence of Jesus' resurrection.

We can look at the example of Great Britain. It's a centuries-old bastion of Christian thought, yet now in modern times, the majority of believers flounder in their fundamental understanding of the resurrection. One in four people who claim to be Christians in the UK even disavow the bodily resurrection of Jesus completely.[1]

But this is incongruent with the faith we see reflected in the Bible. When we open the Scriptures, we see that belief in bodily resurrection powered the early church to turn the world upside down, that resurrection faith was the key to their ethics, that resurrection faith brought hope in moments of worldly despair, and that resurrection faith caused the earliest followers of Jesus to become the greatest force for God on planet Earth.

Indeed, a staggering three hundred verses in the New Testament address the resurrection across its 260 chapters. Author Lee Strobel, my dear friend of many years, often says, "Every single shred of evidence for the resurrection of Jesus Christ is also evidence for my eventual resurrection." And in a death-devastating promise, Jesus guarantees the believer's resurrection: "I am the resurrection and the life; he who believes in me, though he die, yet shall he live" (John 11:25 RSV).

In 1 Corinthians, the apostle Paul is crystal clear about the importance of resurrection faith:

> If Christ has not been raised, then our preaching is in vain and your faith is in vain. We are even found to be misrepresenting God, because we testified of God that he raised Christ, whom he did not raise if it is true that the dead are not raised. For if the dead are not raised, then Christ has not been raised. If Christ has not been raised, your faith is futile and you are still in your sins.
>
> 1 Corinthians 15:14–17 RSV

Then in a radical comparison, he challenges Christians, saying if the historical fact of Jesus' resurrection is false, they should "eat and drink, for tomorrow we die" (1 Corinthians 15:32). In other words, if Jesus didn't rise from the dead, we should live however we please with no margins or guardrails.

And Paul also says our preaching and our faith are "empty" (verse 14 NKJV). Yet the truth of the resurrection of Jesus calls us to holiness and purity of life.

These days it's troubling that churches rarely preach series on Jesus' resurrection. Outside of a funeral or Easter service, believers may go weeks or even months without learning about or considering his resurrection. This lack of teaching, however, is opposite to what we see in the life of the early Christian church. Matthew, Mark, Luke, and John were careful to record "many convincing proofs" (Acts 1:3 NIV) evidencing the bodily resurrection of Jesus. After carefully investigating everything from the beginning, Luke wrote it is possible for us to "have certainty concerning the things you have been taught" about our Christian faith (Luke 1:4). And the resurrection proves we serve a God of second chances.

History tells us something happened to Jesus on that early Sunday morning, something that changed the lives of the people who witnessed it (see Mark 16:14; Luke 24:34–43; John 20:19–31; and Acts 1:3–4, 9:3–6 for some of these post-resurrection appearances, as well as a list of them in chapter 8). On Friday night, the day of the crucifixion, the disciples were running scared. A few days later they were more than willing to endure ridicule, imprisonment, mistreatment, and even death. And in the book of Acts, we see they told the Sanhedrin, "We cannot help speaking about what we have seen and heard" (Acts 4:20 NIV; see also 4:1–3, 18–20).

Christianity, then, is quintessentially a resurrection religion. Yet practically, is it possible that just one morning could have changed the world? Could most, if not all, of life's problems be addressed by an unusual occurrence on a Sunday morning so long ago? Could it be that God's answer to the injustice in our world is exactly what came to us over a thirty-nine-hour period at a Jewish criminal's borrowed tomb in a Roman outpost? Could it be so simple?

In a word, yes. Furthermore, we can—and in this book, we will—learn the most compelling answers to these core questions: *Can we be sure Jesus physically rose from the dead?* and *Does Jesus' resurrection make any difference in our lives today?* The resurrection of Jesus Christ has profound ramifications that are both simple to understand and sophisticated, and it's the seminal issue for the church today even as it was that first Easter in the first century. Nothing is more important for a Christian than Jesus' resurrection, yet it assumes a heavy burden of proof.

Unfortunately, the most important fact of the Christian faith is also the most misunderstood. Most followers of Jesus have a woefully inadequate understanding of his resurrection. They respect the bodily resurrection of Jesus, but few are able to articulate the evidence that supports their belief in his resurrection.

+ + +

Body of Proof presupposes my earlier works and rests on the shoulders of first-rate scholarly mentorship and my PhD research.[2] Just as the Corinthian Christians needed to be reminded of the gospel (1 Corinthians 15), my hope is that this book is a tool you can return to again and again, reminding you of the powerful evidence for the gospel and the transformational difference living a resurrection-centric life makes.

My goal and prayer for this book, then, is to illuminate your heart with the seven best reasons to believe in Jesus' bodily resurrection. I focus on the evidence for resurrection by building a case supporting the Christian belief that Jesus was resurrected on the third day following his crucifixion. I offer a careful and thorough scholarly analysis of the biblical records that pertain to the resurrection of Jesus and conclude that those records are reliable in reporting the resurrection of Jesus. And I critique alternative theories that have been proposed to explain away the accuracy of the biblical narrative of the resurrection of Jesus.

I invite you, then, to travel back in time with me to a particular weekend. Little did everyone there know it would include executions, an earthquake, daytime darkness, an uprising, and a transformational miracle the likes of which the world had never seen.

+ + +

A final word before we begin:

Jesus' bodily resurrection secures our future with hope. In fact, the Bible teaches us that in Christ we have a "living hope" (1 Peter 1:3) and a "sure" hope (Hebrews 6:19).

Although I'm not from a liturgical background, I've always admired the affirmation of the "sure and certain hope of the resurrection" in the Committal Prayer:

> In sure and certain hope of the resurrection to eternal life through our Lord Jesus Christ, we commend to Almighty God our brother____; and we commit his body to the ground; earth to earth, ashes to ashes, dust to dust. The Lord bless him and keep him, the Lord make his face to shine upon him and be gracious unto him, the Lord lift up his countenance upon him and give him peace. Amen.

While writing this book, never far from my mind was a specific family that has experienced the worst grief. My little sister, Jenilee, and her husband, Jeff Mullikin, experienced the tragic loss of their son, Wesley, stillborn at twenty-five weeks. My hope is that the truths offered in *Body of Proof* will bring encouragement to Jenilee and Jeff with the rock-solid promise that they will hold Wesley in their arms someday soon. Painful as it has been, the good-bye is only temporary, and so our family grieves in hope.

Perhaps you've experienced life-changing grief. If so, Jesus' resurrection will bring you hope and healing. Or you may be reeling from disappointment or discouragement. If so, my prayer is that Jesus' resurrection will strengthen your heart and steady your path. But like me, you may need to be convinced in your heart through the mind. So let me take you on this journey that will leave you intellectually stimulated and spiritually enlightened by the transforming truth of Jesus' resurrection.

More, I pray that as you read, the Holy Spirit will inspire you with a new or renewed faith in Jesus' resurrection—and in your own. May we forever praise the Lord Jesus, for he is not behind us in a tomb but before us on a throne.

PART ONE

SKEPTICS TAKE
the MICROPHONE

1

"Isn't the Resurrection
Imaginative Storytelling?"

The email caught me by surprise. Sam Roberts, a writer for the *New York Times*, was reaching out to a group of scholars, asking us to participate in a fascinating project: writing a contemporary, serious obituary for Jesus that could have appeared at the time of his death.

I was delighted to accept Sam's invitation and add my insights to those from the other scholars. And a few months later, the obituary was published on Easter weekend in *Vanity Fair*.

Jesus of Nazareth, Whose Messianic Message
Captivated Thousands, Dies at About 33

Jesus of Nazareth, a Galilean carpenter turned itinerant minister whose appeals to piety and whose repute as a healer had galvanized a growing contingent of believers, died on Friday after being crucified that morning just outside Jerusalem, only days after his followers had welcomed him triumphantly to the city as "the anointed one" and "the Son of David." He was about 33.

For a man who had lived the first three decades of his life in virtual obscurity, he attracted a remarkable following in only a few years.

His reputation reflected a persuasive coupling of message, personal magnetism, and avowed miracles. But it also resonated in the current moment of spiritual and economic discontent and popular resentment of authority and privilege, whether wielded by foreigners from Rome or by the Jewish priests in Jerusalem and their confederates.

Still, Jesus had been preceded in recent years by a litany of false messiahs. He followed a roster of self-styled prophets who promised salvation and, with their ragtag followers from separatist sects, cults, and fractious rebel groups, were branded as bandits by the governing Romans, ostracized by the ruling priests as heretics in a period of pessimistic apocalyptic expectation, and already lost to history.

Despite the throngs that greeted him in Jerusalem and applauded his daring assault on the Temple and his attack on the money changers who operate within its precincts with impunity, it is arguable whether the legacy of this man—whom some contemporaries dismissed, if guardedly, as "the one they call Messiah"—will be any more enduring or his followers any more committed than the prophets and their devotees who preceded him.

(Moreover, what he might have accomplished further had he lived is also debatable, since the average life span today is not much more than 40.)

Jesus seems to have been universally respected as a wise man whose appeal for mercy, humility, and compassion reverberated powerfully. But he left no written record, and, according to those who heard him, he sometimes preached mixed messages. He would bless the peacemakers, but also suggest that his followers buy swords. He would insist that his mission was solely to minister to "the lost sheep of the house of Israel," but would also direct his devotees to proselytize to other nations.

Even less is known about Jesus' youth. He was born Yeshua bar Joseph (his very name, "Yahweh saves," or freedom, after Joshua, could be considered incitable), in all likelihood in Nazareth (he was known as "the Nazarean"). Some adherents, however, insist that he was born in Bethlehem, a claim that would polish his bona fides as an heir to King David.

His father was named Joseph, although references to him are scarce after Jesus' birth. His mother was Miriam, or Mary, and because he was sometimes referred to as "Mary's son," questions had been raised about his paternity.

He is believed to have been the eldest of at least six siblings, including four brothers—James, Joseph, Judas, and Simon—and several sisters. He never married—unusual for a man of his age, but not surprising for a Jew with an apocalyptic vision.

His survivors include his mother, his brother James, and a number of other siblings.

His family was devoutly Jewish, probably one of a hundred or so Jewish families in a windswept, mostly mud-and-brick hilltop village in lower Galilee populated largely by peasants and laborers. Although it is only an hour's walk from cosmopolitan Sepphoris, the Nazareth in which he was born still remains unidentified on most maps, an indication of its insignificance.

Jesus spoke Aramaic, probably with a smattering of Hebrew and Greek, but although Nazareth had a synagogue, there is no record of his having had access to a formal education.

He grew up in a turbulent time. King Herod the Great had managed to pacify rival groups of Jews, Arabs, Greeks, Samaritans, and Syrians on behalf of the territory occupied by Rome for nearly six decades. But Herod's death, roughly the same year that Jesus was born, and the completion of the Temple in Jerusalem contributed to mass unemployment, which further widened the gap in economic inequality that Jesus would witness growing up.

In his late 20s, Jesus was drawn to an ascetic preacher named John, who initiated his followers into what he believed was the true nation of Israel. According to John's custom, they repented their sins and purged their impurities in the Jordan River, an immersion ritual commonly known in Hebrew as a mikveh and transliterated from Greek as baptisma.

Jesus was baptized shortly before John the Baptist's explosive popularity rattled the skittish Romans, who arrested and executed him.

Even before that, though, Jesus had begun his own ministry, referring to himself as rabbi or teacher, citing the scriptures, which suggested he was literate, but also speaking in original parables.

He was accompanied eventually by a dozen disciples, mirroring the 12 tribes of Israel. He was unusually receptive to women, and forgiving to sinners (those who flouted God's commandments rather than priestly rituals) and even to reviled tax collectors (despite his anti-establishment rhetoric, he acknowledged the right of Rome to collect taxes).

His following, of mostly Jewish and Greek heritage (he even converted contemptuous Samaritans) grew as word of the miracles he had performed spread before him.

These miracles mirrored those performed by earlier Jewish prophets in the Hebrew Bible, although Jesus was said by his followers to have outdone his predecessors. Elijah, in one instance, was said to have employed three prayers and some theatrics to raise a child from the dead; Jesus reputedly did it with just a word. Elisha, in another, was said to have fed 100 people with 20 barley loaves; Jesus was credited with feeding 5,000 with 5 loaves.

Supported largely by the hospitality of benefactors in Capernaum, on the Sea of Galilee, Jesus avoided large cities on his pilgrimage of preaching, which culminated last week in his arrival in Jerusalem.

It is believed that he timed his arrival to occur on the eve of Passover, when the city's population swells to celebrate a holiday rife with contemporary symbolism: the Jews' salvation from foreign subjugation.

After running afoul of the Jewish elite in Jerusalem for blasphemy and his arrest on Thursday, Jesus was sentenced to death by Governor Pontius Pilate. (The Jewish authorities lacked jurisdiction to impose capital punishment.) The charge, in effect, was treason, for claiming to be King of the Jews or "the anointed one" (Messiah in Hebrew and Aramaic; Christos in Greek).

After he was declared dead on Friday night, he was buried nearby in a cave. On Sunday, his disciples reported that the body was missing.[1]

Given the vastly different perspectives of those who contributed to Jesus' obituary, I was unsure how Sam would conclude it. I was pleased he ended with a cliffhanger: *On Sunday, his disciples reported that the body was missing.* But where do we go from here? From the mystery about what happened next to the assurance that Jesus was indeed resurrected?

The Historical Test

In Sam's query to the contributors, I especially appreciated his two questions: *Is there enough to say?* and *What sources should I consult?* This gets at a subtle but sophisticated point. Unlike any other religion, Christianity put itself to the historical test through explicit interaction with history in the Roman Empire of the first century. Many often miss this point: No other religion comes close to Christianity in that you can test it against history. My contribution to Sam's obituary project was to evidentially travel back in time to that first Easter in first-century Jerusalem.

Dating based between Caiaphas's removal from office as high priest (AD 36), Pilate's governorship (AD 26–36), as well as on the annual Jewish Passover (Jewish month of Nisan) provides a solid evidential basis to peg the crucifixion and resurrection on April 7–9, AD 30 (April 3–5, AD 33, are alternative dates).

The Jewish calendar was based on lunar months, and the astronomical calculations provide only two options for Nisan 14 between AD 26 and AD 36. The forecast would have called for warmer weather. The city of Jerusalem would have been brimming over with Jews who had descended on the city for the annual Passover festival.

Jesus' death by Roman crucifixion is the best established fact of the ancient world. If we can't believe Jesus of Nazareth died by Roman crucifixion, we can't believe anything about the ancient world. So embolden your faith knowing that in researching the life of Jesus, one must appeal to Roman emperors to find equal documentation.

I find this point fascinating. There is a great deal of evidence for Jesus, both for his public life and his public execution. Only the Roman emperors themselves are better attested in history.[2] I often start here when talking with skeptics and seekers alike. The documentation is the most objective evidence we have outside the Bible. It is not theory or hypothesis. Everyone can weigh the evidence for themselves.

When we study any historical event, we look to early eyewitness testimony. In other words, we assume the closer we get to the actual event, the more accurate the testimony. It turns out that, evidentially, we can reach back to within six weeks of the resurrection, which is astounding.

The apostles did not receive the gospel secondhand but "were eyewitnesses of the word" (Luke 1:2), which they received personally from Jesus Christ. The word *eyewitnesses* is from the Greek word *autoptes*, similar to our medical term *autopsy*. Luke, then, a physician, used a medical descriptor for their detailed examination of the risen Christ.

Indeed, Jesus' body was missing from the tomb and the disciples were spreading the news. Soon, some of the fiercest critics would agree that Jesus' resurrection was real. According to first-century historian Josephus, James, the brother of Jesus, moved from cynic to proclaiming his belief in Jesus as the Messiah, martyred for that faith in AD 62. Can you imagine believing your brother is the Son of God? Would you be willing to die proclaiming your faith in the resurrected Messiah?

My pastor, Dr. Jack Graham, has said, "The day you see Jesus will be the best day of your life."[3] In all I've read and studied related to the resurrection, I must admit that I'd never thought of seeing Jesus as the best day of my life, but now I do. Dr. Graham is right. This changed my perspective and gave me a renewed energy to complete this book and continue "proclaiming in Jesus the resurrection of the dead" (Acts 4:2).

Let me first take you to Oxford, England, where I defended my 93,000-word dissertation on the resurrection of Jesus.

"Do You Believe?"

"Do you *believe* the resurrection of Jesus happened? Or is it imaginative storytelling?"

That's how one of the finest Bible scholars in Britain, Professor William Telford, started my *viva voce*—my PhD defense. The pressure was on. This was it. I swallowed hard, butterflies in my stomach. No do-overs are offered when pursuing a PhD in the United Kingdom, where on this December midafternoon the sun was already beginning to set at Oxford. It was pass or fail. No do-overs. Full stop.

"Professor Telford, David Hume said wise men choose probabilities," I answered, not breaking eye contact with him. "The evidence leads me to believe that, yes, Jesus physically, bodily rose from the dead."

"I *don't* see it that way," Telford replied, responding to me as one with experience—made even more authoritative by his wearing a perfectly tied bow tie and clutching reading glasses. Then gently smiling as he shook his head, he said, "Let's begin your viva."

This was not a Bible study group or a conversation at a local coffee shop. This was my doctoral defense. Three years earlier at RIS (Research Induction School), for six weeks I was taught it didn't matter what I personally believed. In fact, it was *irrelevant* to my research in a British doctoral program. I was taught to be a dispassionate researcher. I was instructed not to "privilege" the text of the Bible based on my beliefs. Nobody cared what I believed—or so my tutors said.

Now, fast-forwarding three years, I had written a 93,000-word doctoral thesis focused on the resurrection of Jesus, and the first question asked at my examination was about what I believed.

What did I believe?

The more we know about our faith, the calmer we are in a faith dialogue and the better we listen. I was generally nervous regarding my viva, to be sure; however, I wasn't nervous or unsure about what I believed. I had studied the most strident arguments against the resurrection of Jesus and walked into my viva in Oxford more iron-fisted about following the physically, bodily resurrected Jesus than at any other time in my life. Yes, Jesus physically, bodily rose from the dead—and the evidence led me to a stronger belief.

When those words of affirming belief left my mouth, the peace of God filled my heart. I was ready for my examination. Professor Telford, who had the unique ability to speak Latin and English in the same sentence, might disagree with my personal decisions, but he would not be able to shoot down my arguments, methodology, and academic conclusion.

I'm thankful that my doctoral advisor, Professor Craig Evans, considered the finest Jesus scholar in the English-speaking world, agreed to fly to Oxford with me and be present to observe the viva. Professor Evans was equally surprised to hear Telford's opening question. My ability and conviction to answer the man's cross-examination would, in large part, determine the course of my future scholarship, ministry, and personal walk with Christ. The stakes could not have been higher.

Three hours or so later, Professor Telford passed me with commendation and encouraged publication of my thesis in a respected academic monograph series. In a moment, I became *Dr.* Johnston. (For more about my academic path leading to this and other writings, see "From Oxford to Jerusalem—My Academic Journey" at the back of this book.)

Since earning my PhD, I've presented more than one hundred lectures on the resurrection, and that experience has revealed that I have two strikes against me whenever I present the evidential body of proof for the resurrection of Jesus: (1) I'm persuaded that the New Testament is a historical document and we should study the resurrection of Jesus the same way we research any other historical event, and (2) I believe the historical fact of Jesus' resurrection has the most explanatory power.

These two strikes are expected yet not insurmountable. But make no mistake about it, we're living in a post-Christian— and at times even hostile to anything Jesus-related—culture. It's doing its best to convince the world there's nothing special about Jesus: *If he even existed, he was just a normal guy with a wife, kids, and the first-century equivalent to a mortgage.* Or, *Later, people who didn't even know Jesus turned him into a divine being and created imaginative stories about him.* These are popular hot takes today.

Compounding the problem is the rank Bible and history illiteracy among many followers of Jesus who have never moved beyond their Sunday school understanding of his victorious resurrection from the dead. Easter means not much more to them than chocolate rabbits and decorated eggs.

If you were cross-examined about why you believe in the physical, bodily resurrection of Jesus, what evidence would you offer without flinching? If you were in my position and someone

31

asked if the resurrection was simply "imaginative storytelling," how would you respond?

For any of us to give a fully formed and persuasive reply, we first need to review the case against Jesus' resurrection. And the debaters, lawyers, professors, educators, journalists, and media who read this book know we must first understand the dissenters' claims. That's what we'll explore next.

2

The Case against Jesus' Resurrection

The case against the resurrection of Jesus is usually based on the utter uniqueness of the claim itself: A man who had been dead for two or three days came back to life. Skeptics also usually claim that the historical evidence itself is weak, that there were no witnesses of the event or the New Testament writings that report the resurrection are not credible.

It's not hard to understand why many are skeptical. As an illustration, one can imagine excited family members and friends claiming that their beloved uncle Ralph, who died and was buried a few days ago, is now alive and has appeared to them. Almost no one would believe such a report, assuming that it was either part of a hoax or that some grotesque mistake had been made—that Uncle Ralph had not actually died but was buried alive and later awoke in the mausoleum (apparently not embalmed as we would expect in modern times). Even if a team of medical doctors gave testimony that the man really was dead when buried, most of us would remain skeptical. Surely there's a better explanation for the apparent resurrection of Uncle Ralph than a literal resurrection.

The natural inclination toward skepticism lies behind most theories that have in various ways sought to refute the claims of the resurrection of Jesus. A number of them attempt to provide coherent and compelling alternative explanations. With the exception of *mythicists* (discussed briefly below), historians readily concede the following facts with respect to Jesus:

- He lived, he was a public figure, and he was surrounded by a number of disciples who were trained to carry on the activities and teachings of Jesus.
- He was publicly put to death on a Roman cross.
- Within a short time after his death, his followers proclaimed that he'd been raised up and was living in a new and transformed way (that is, he was resurrected).
- Believers and unbelievers alike can agree on the historical fact that the disciples had experiences of seeing Jesus after his death.[1]

Christians believe that the actual resurrection of Jesus is the best explanation for these historical givens. Skeptics, however, have offered a number of explanations that don't require the conclusion that Jesus was literally raised from the dead. Most of these explanations have no following today, but it will be helpful to review them briefly. They fall into two broad categories: misconception and deceit.

Misconception Theories

Theories of misconception usually take one of two forms: either Jesus didn't die or his followers visited the wrong tomb.

The idea that Jesus didn't die on the cross but was taken down and buried while still alive is usually called the *swoon theory*. It supposes that Jesus passed out, perhaps becoming comatose; that his executioners wrongly thought he was dead; and that his followers who buried him also wrongly thought he was dead. Then after a day or two in the tomb, Jesus awoke, managed to exit the tomb, and found a few of his followers. Then the story quickly spread with the followers of Jesus assuming wrongly that Jesus had been raised from the dead.

The reason almost no one today finds the swoon theory compelling is that it's beset with several improbabilities. First, it's unlikely that Jesus was removed from the cross while still alive. And if he was, it's not likely that he would revive in the tomb and manage to escape.

Furthermore, even if it's agreed that Jesus might have been buried alive and then managed to exit the tomb, it's most unlikely that anyone seeing the badly wounded Jesus would have thought of him as resurrected and transformed. It's more likely they would have viewed him for what he would have been: a man sorely in need of medical attention.

Furthermore, the swoon theory does not account for the testimony of Saul of Tarsus, later known as Paul, who a year or two after the crucifixion met the risen Jesus and was converted from an enemy of the Christian movement to an energetic proponent. It's highly improbable that had he met a recovered Jesus who had not experienced a physical transformation, Saul would have thought of him as resurrected or divine.

The second alternative explanation that assumes a misconception is the well-known *wrong tomb theory*, proposed a century ago. According to this theory, yes, some of Jesus' female followers went to the tomb early Sunday morning to anoint his body and mourn. But not knowing in which tomb his body had been placed, they went to the wrong one. A gardener or custodian, recognizing their confusion, simply told the women that Jesus was "not here." The women, the theory goes, misunderstood this encounter, believing the man to be an angel declaring that Jesus had "risen," that he was no longer in the grave but had been taken up into heaven. The lack of a body in the tomb they'd mistakenly visited confirmed their misunderstanding. The women then began proclaiming the resurrection of Jesus.

No one today holds to the wrong tomb theory for several reasons. For one, it assumes a rather low opinion of Jesus' followers. Is it likely that none of them would have ever discovered that the tomb visited by the women was in fact not the tomb of Jesus?

Most of those who advanced this theory were unacquainted with Jewish burial traditions and tombs in first-century Jerusalem, but archaeologists and historians now have a better understanding of Jewish burial practices in the time of Jesus. They include carefully marking not only the tomb but the very niche in the tomb where the corpse had been placed in anticipation of the gathering and reburial of the bones by family members one year later. This sacred duty in Jewish burial traditions is known as ossilegium, the placement of the bones of the deceased into an ossuary.

Another reason the wrong tomb theory is unpersuasive is that it doesn't account for Jesus' appearances to Peter and Paul. In the case of Paul, we have several authentic letters in which he describes his encounter with the risen Jesus. Correctly identifying the tomb where the body of Jesus had been placed plays no part in Paul's experience.

A variation of the misconception approach is seen in recent psychological explanations, conceding that Peter and Paul and perhaps others may have actually experienced visions of Jesus. Some suggest these experiences were *intramental* (in the mind) in that they were purely subjective. These new theories represent an updated version of the much older *hallucination theory*, in which it was thought that the disciples only imagined seeing Jesus, which then gave rise to the idea that he'd been raised from the dead. Indeed, as early as the second century, Celsus and other critics of the resurrection proclamation suggested hallucination, brought on by wishful thinking (more about them in later chapters).

The psychological alternative theory is in vogue today in some circles, but it enjoys no support from the scientific literature for there is no evidence that two or more people could experience the same hallucination. Even if, for the sake of argument, it is conceded that Peter and others who knew Jesus intimately might have had such hallucinations (similar to the experiences of the widowed who imagine seeing their late spouses), it's extremely unlikely that a nonfollower—indeed, an enemy—like Saul of Tarsus would have had the same intramental experience.

Deceit Theories

Some theorists have contended that belief in the resurrection of Jesus was a result of deceit on the part of his followers. One approach is to suggest that stories of resurrection didn't begin to circulate until many years after Jesus' death. Most thinkers today, though, recognize that this hardly explains the sudden emergence of the church after Jesus' death nor Paul's sudden conversion, the latter, again, occurring only a year or two after Jesus' death. Accordingly, some claim that some of Jesus' disciples made up the resurrection story soon after his death. Initially, they say, the empty tomb played no part; followers of Jesus simply proclaimed the resurrection. And later, the fictional story of women visiting the tomb and finding it empty began to circulate.

The problem with these theories of deceit is that they fly in the face of Jesus' ethical teaching. Is it probable that the followers of such a teacher would lie in such an extraordinary fashion? And if so, to what end? As Jews, they held to a coherent theistic faith (regarded as superior to pagan polytheism), which included hope for life after death. If in dying the way he did Jesus was apparently defeated and his message falsified, then why create the story of a resurrection? Why rehabilitate an apparent failed prophet and Messiah? Why claim against all popular expectations that the crucified Jesus was Israel's long-awaited Messiah? The scenario is improbable.

In the last century, including in recent years, a number of other complicated theories of deceit have been proposed. These usually entail a conspiracy involving the Jewish high priest, the Roman governor, one or more of the disciples, Luke the physician, or others. According to these theories, Jesus' death is faked; he is buried, then later helped from his tomb; he is revived, tricked out in impressive apparel; and then he appears to various gullible disciples, convincing them that he is indeed resurrected. No credible historian has embraced theories of this type.

One more way to deny the resurrection is to claim that Jesus was not in fact a person of history. This approach has been called *mythicism*. Mythicists claim that the historical evidence for Jesus is weak, well below the threshold we should expect of someone so notable if the New Testament Gospels really do speak of a person who lived and had contemporary followers.

Mythicism is regarded as eccentric, and this view is held by almost no historian or credible scholar. The evidence for the existence of a historical person known as Jesus, from the Galilean village of Nazareth, who was a public figure for a year or two and then after a confrontation with authorities in Jerusalem died on a Roman cross is substantial. Not only were four biographies written and circulated within one or two generations of his time, but we have the letters of Paul, a contemporary, who knew some of Jesus' original followers (including Peter and John) and was acquainted with Jesus' brother James.

Almost all scholars accept as authentic several of Paul's letters, including 1 Corinthians and Galatians. In these letters Paul not only refers to James, the brother of Jesus, but claims to have met him, along with two or three of Jesus' original followers—for example, Peter and John. No one doubts that Paul was a contemporary of these men. The idea that he could be talking about a brother of Jesus and the original followers of Jesus and yet this Jesus was not a real person strikes many as absurd.

Some mythicists go so far as to claim that there was no village called Nazareth in the early first century, that Christians invented it along with Jesus himself. No archaeologist agrees with such an extreme hypothesis. Indeed, they point to a fourth-century Jewish inscription found at Caesarea Maritima (a major city on Israel's Mediterranean coast where the Roman governors resided), which lists courses (groups) of priests, including those of Nazareth. I know many archaeologists—Jewish, Christian, and of no religious orientation whatsoever—and not one doubts that Jesus was a real person. Indeed, the vast majority of these archaeologists view the Gospels as providing valuable historical data. Fictitious narratives about a mythical figure from a nonexistent village would not exhibit the reality that archaeologists and historians find in the New Testament Gospels.

Accordingly, mainstream scholars accept the historical authenticity of Jesus, and so should we.

PART TWO

The RESURRECTION BEARS *a* HEAVY BURDEN *of* PROOF

3

The Christian Claim That Jesus Was Resurrected

Shifting away from the death and resurrection of Jesus Christ is a growing movement within the church. Too many so-called followers are focused on humanizing Jesus to such an extent that he is no longer divine. Instead, they say, he was simply a great moral teacher—a nice person who turned the other cheek and loved his enemies. A growing number of "Christians," then, are unable to say that Jesus' resurrection is significant or even matters.

Yet when we look to the source material for Christianity, we see that not only did Jesus make some radical claims while on earth, but most scholars would agree with those claims. Even skeptics, at minimum, agree that

- Jesus thought of himself as having an intimate relationship with God,
- Jesus believed he had been chosen by God to usher in God's kingdom, and

- Jesus believed himself to be a miracle worker and exorcist—and he did deeds to back up his claims.

His critics, then, were saying—and rightly so—"Well, if you're this person you claim to be, show us a sign." And Jesus responded, "I will give you one sign: my resurrection from the dead" (see Matthew 12:38–42).

The bottom line is this: If Jesus did not rise from the dead, that makes him a false prophet unworthy of our allegiance and no rational person should follow. But if Jesus did rise from the dead, it seems to me that he did so in confirmation of his personal and radical claims. And that gives us something to think about, which is exactly what happened to the first Christians.

The heart of the Christian gospel is the bodily resurrection of Jesus of Nazareth. Even so, the claim that he was truly resurrected assumes a heavy burden of proof. To suggest that he was not resurrected, however, one must account for the origin and emergence of resurrection traditions with a "mythmaking" model.

As we learned in the previous chapter, the mythmaking approach to the life of Jesus is intellectually incoherent. If Jesus was a myth, so was the Roman Empire. Yet this can't explain the complaints voiced by early objectors of these accounts (see Matthew 12). If Jesus is a myth like Santa Claus or the tooth fairy, why are skeptical thinkers writing hardcore arguments against Jesus, his resurrection, and his early followers?

In my book *Unanswered*, I wrote,

Why did Jesus' followers think he had been resurrected? What persuaded them? It would have been much easier, and certainly more culturally palatable, to proclaim that Jesus was a ghostly apparition. In his Pentecost sermon, Peter proclaimed, "This Jesus God raised up, and of that we are all witnesses" (Acts 2:32). It's noteworthy that Peter points out that they "all" were witnesses. This testimony of a bodily resurrection, not a ghostly apparition, was not a rumor. It was not vague, third-hand hearsay. Rather, it was known by eyewitnesses and seen by "all." Who could dispute it? Where were the voices of the objectors? The resurrected Jesus was seen and experienced by his own disciples and dozens of others.

Notice it was the women who observed the place where Jesus was buried. (Mark 15:47.) All four Gospel writers report that it was women—the same women who supported Jesus during his earthly ministry (Luke 8)—who first witnessed the empty tomb. The Lukan tradition portrays at least five women—two Marys and Joanna—and adds "the other women" (Luke 24:10) without any more specificity.[1]

Resurrection Ideas from Jesus and among His Contemporaries

Jesus not only believed in resurrection but taught it. When emissaries from John the Baptist asked if he was the awaited "one who is to come," he responded, "The blind receive their sight and the lame walk, lepers are cleansed and the deaf hear, and the dead are raised up, and the poor have good news preached to them" (Matthew 11:3, 5; see also Luke 7:22). The declaration "the dead are raised up" refers to actual resuscitations but also anticipates the resurrection.

According to Josephus, John the Baptist was Herod Antipas's prisoner in the stronghold known as Machaerus in the region of Perea. This is the place where Herod would have John beheaded.[2] Jesus responds to John's doubt by providing evidence of resurrection miracles associated with his Messiahship.

Some Jewish individuals and groups in the approximate time of Jesus did not believe in resurrection. Best known among them were the Sadducees, a small, aristocratic group well represented among the ruling priests in the late Second Temple period. The New Testament Gospels tell of an encounter between Jesus and the Sadducees—"who say there is no resurrection" (Matthew 20:23). Appealing to the story of Moses and the burning bush, Jesus defends the doctrine (Matthew 22:23–33; Mark 12:18–27; Luke 20:27–40).

Josephus, who, again, was a first-century Jewish historian and apologist, described the views of the Pharisees, Sadducees, and Essenes. He wrote that the Pharisees believed the human soul is imperishable and "passes into another body."[3] It's likely that Josephus was referring to resurrection. In contrast to pharisaic opinion, the Sadducees didn't believe in postmortem judgment or existence of any kind. This sharp difference of opinion between Pharisees and Sadducees lies behind Paul's provocative declaration before the Jewish Council: "With respect to the hope and the resurrection of the dead I am on trial" (Acts 23:6 RSV).

According to Josephus, the Essenes viewed the soul as trapped in the physical body, from which it is released at death and is "borne aloft."[4] One wonders if Josephus was presenting the Essene view in a Greek light. The book of Daniel and related materials were popular at Qumran, the site where the Dead Sea Scrolls the Essenes curated were found, so one would think the resurrection passage in Daniel 12:2 would have been authoritative in Essene beliefs about the end of the world—their eschatology. Perhaps afterlife beliefs at Qumran—Josephus notwithstanding—weren't much different from the ideas held by Pharisees.

The Judeo-Christian Origins of Resurrection

Resurrection in Judeo-Christian tradition is rooted in Jewish Hebrew scripture. In his vision of the restoration of Israel, the prophet Ezekiel describes a valley of dry bones regaining their flesh and becoming living people. Although only metaphor, the vision likely contributed to resurrection ideas.

In the book of Isaiah, we find an oracle that says, "Thy dead shall live, their bodies shall rise. O dwellers in the dust, awake and sing for joy!" (Isaiah 26:19 RSV). This verse, which may have been only poetic, becomes a prophecy in the book of Daniel that quite literally anticipates the resurrection of the dead: "Many of those who sleep in the dust of the earth shall awake, some to everlasting life, and some to shame and everlasting contempt" (Daniel 12:2). The book of Hosea's oracle of national restoration may also have contributed to the hope of resurrection: "After two days he will revive us; on the third day he will raise us up, that we may live before him" (Hosea 6:2).

In later literature, resurrection hopes are clearly expressed. For example, one of the brothers martyred during the pogrom of Antiochus IV in the second century BC says to the tyrant, "You accursed wretch, you dismiss us from this present life, but the King of the universe will raise us up to an everlasting renewal of life" (2 Maccabees 7:9, from the Apocrypha published in the Revised Standard Version of the Bible). At least one text from Qumran speaks of the dead being "made alive."[5]

During the time of Jesus, the religious-political party of the Pharisees held to belief in bodily resurrection (Acts 23:6–8), a view that was accepted by Jesus and his disciples (Mark 12:18–27; Acts 4:2). The apostle Paul affirms the bodily resurrection of Jesus and discusses the implications for those who believe in him (1 Corinthians 15). Jesus followed in the tradition expanding from Daniel to the Pharisees, teaching that there would be a twofold resurrection: the righteous to their reward and the wicked to their judgment. The New Testament writers alluded to, cited, reinterpreted, and developed Jewish texts in light of the eschatological beliefs set in motion after Jesus' resurrection.

The Gospel writers record Jesus' belief in the resurrection in two areas that go hand in hand but are not the same. First, resurrection is an eschatological teaching, an act of God sometime in the future. Jesus cites Exodus 3:6: "I am the God of your father, the God of Abraham, and the God of Isaac, and the God of Jacob," then adds his interpretation: "He is not the God of the dead, but of the living. You are quite wrong" (Mark 12:18–27; see also Matthew 22:23–33; Luke 20:27–40) in reply to the Sadducees, demonstrating his belief in the resurrection.[6] According to Jesus, Abraham continues to exist and to enjoy the blessings of God's covenant. From Jesus' perspective, Abraham would eventually be raised from the dead.

Luke's account of this presents an interesting redactional change. The teachers of the Law (scribes) actually praise Jesus for his answer to the Sadducees: "Then some of the scribes answered, 'Teacher, you have spoken well'" (Luke 20:39). This is perhaps the only passage where the scribes admire or approve of Jesus and his teachings. Matthew 22:33 states that the crowds "were astonished." The reactions from them and the scribes, as recorded by the Gospel writers, show something of the intrigue of resurrection traditions in the first century AD.[7]

Second, Jesus' belief in resurrection can be observed in the canonical Gospels by the resurrection miracles he performs, which we'll cover in chapter 6, "Reason #3: Jesus Demonstrated Resurrection Power."

Resurrection deeds were also understood to possess messianic significance. We see this in Jesus' response to John's question ("Are you the one who is to come?" in Matthew 11:3) and in the way Matthew introduced the exchange in verse 2: "Now when John heard in prison about the deeds of the Christ . . ." In Jesus' reply in verse 5, he alludes to healing, raising the dead, and proclaiming goods news to the oppressed taking place with the appearance of God's Messiah. This remarkable saying (also in Luke 7:22) not only affirms Jesus' belief in resurrection but confirms his own messianic role in it.[8]

Consequently, the language of resurrection, not to mention deeds that Jesus and his contemporaries viewed as actual instances of "being raised up" (whether "resuscitation" or "resurrection"), almost certainly charged the disciples prior to Easter with ideas that came into play on Easter and in the days that followed. In what ways they made distinctions between these events—especially in comparison with the Easter event itself—is not easy to determine, but it is a question that must be addressed.

How do we find the real Jesus and transcend all the distortions being tossed around in our culture? Let's look at what the real Jesus taught, did, and achieved.

What Did the Real Jesus Teach?

In the real Gospels—the first-century Gospels—we discover that Jesus proclaimed the kingdom of God. He said this kingdom had come, and that it makes a difference for eternity. You won't find that teaching in the Gospel of Thomas, the Gospel of Peter, or some of these other "extra-canonical gospels." You certainly won't find it in any of the gospels not included in the New Testament canon. The real Jesus taught that he is more powerful than Satan, and he demonstrated that with exorcisms.

Jesus also taught that One wiser and greater than Solomon was here. Solomon was famous in the Jewish world of Jesus' time, so that was an amazing claim. He also taught that he had authority to forgive sin—another amazing claim. "Who is this man who even forgives sins?" the Pharisees asked (Luke 7:49 HCSB). Now, *that* is someone with authority from heaven. That is what the four New Testament Gospels teach. That is what the real Jesus taught.

What Did the Real Jesus Do?

Jesus reached out and forgave sinners. He summoned and empowered disciples. He challenged the calloused and indifferent. He rebuked hypocrites and phonies. He warned apostates—those who had fallen away—of coming judgment. He surrendered his life in order to fulfill the will of his Father in heaven. You won't find the Jesus who did those things in any of the extracanonical gospels. In fact, you will discover that sin is no big deal in these other gospels.

Sin is no big deal in some circles today as well, and that's why many people are attracted to these extracanonical gospels. They mirror their thinking. Not everybody wants Jesus to be Lord. Not everyone wants to be held accountable. The phony Jesus claimed by many people today is a much compromised Jesus.

What Did the Real Jesus Achieve?

Jesus revealed the true God in his fullness. "Anyone who has seen me has seen the Father," he explained to his disciples (John 14:9 NIV). The real Jesus died on the cross for sinners, making forgiveness possible. The Jesus of the extracanonical gospels did not die on the cross. There is no talk of forgiveness of sin; in fact, these gospels go out of their way to suggest that something else happened. The second-century heretic Basilides suggested that Jesus fooled everybody by trading places with Simon of Cyrene.

Talk about having a bad day! According to Basilides, Simon of Cyrene showed up for the Passover, and the next thing he knew, he was asked to carry Jesus' cross. Jesus then slipped away in the crowd, and everybody thought Simon was Jesus. So poor Simon was nailed to the cross, and Jesus sneaked away laughing.

As crazy as that story may sound, a similar story is repeated in the Qur'an today.[9] That's why Muslims say Jesus was not put to death by the Jews. But the real Jesus of the New Testament Gospels was crucified, died a real death, and was raised in a real resurrection on the third day, thus confirming all he taught and proving that his life and death were approved by

God. His sacrifice was indeed acceptable. And it would not need to be repeated.

That is what the real Jesus achieved. The phony Jesus did none of those things. The phony Jesus offers no hope. In fact, the phony Jesus is quite diverse. There are all kinds of phony Jesuses.

How Did the New Testament Writers Remember What Jesus Said and Did?

How did Matthew remember the Sermon on the Mount and accurately record it in his Gospel? How was Dr. Luke able to transcribe the words of Peter's Pentecost sermon in Acts? How could the writers remember everything for so many years before it was recorded? We believe the Gospels are eyewitness accounts, but why did the eyewitnesses take thirty to forty years to write their accounts?

These are great questions, but the very fact that they're raised reflects a modern way of thinking. We're looking at the New Testament through twenty-first-century glasses.

If the president of the United States says something, we can read about it almost immediately, somewhere on the internet, on a breaking news site or popular social media app. It would seem strange to us if somebody said, "Someone will write down the president's speech in about twenty years. But for now we'll just pass it along by word of mouth." We live in an age of instant information. What's happening in the world is literally at our fingertips.

But that was not Jesus' world. When Jesus spoke in the first century, his purpose was not for someone to record his words. He taught, repeated his message, and expressed his teachings using new words in a new context. And in doing so, he showed that the message was adaptable and he expected his disciples to learn it, repeat it, and apply it in their own ways. Jesus didn't write down his sermon and then read it. That is a modern approach.

The first century, then, was an oral culture. That's the way things were done. People were used to listening to what someone taught and remembering it. The verbal story of someone who experienced an event had more value than the written word; it was seen as a living voice.

Why did it take so long for the Gospels to be written? Because people didn't start writing them down until these witnesses, these living voices, began to die. Soon they wouldn't have eyewitnesses around to tell the stories orally.

The apostles oversaw this oral tradition. When Judas was replaced, the requirement was that the new apostle had to be someone who'd been with Jesus from the beginning. He had to have known Jesus personally:

> Therefore it is necessary to choose one of the men who have been with us the whole time the Lord Jesus was living among us, beginning from John's baptism to the time when Jesus was taken up from us. For one of these must become a witness with us of his resurrection.
>
> Acts 1:21–22 NIV

We know from Scripture that Jesus gave the Sermon on the Mount, but he probably taught the same type of message frequently as he traveled from place to place. His followers would have heard this teaching over and over, remembered it, and eventually memorialized it in writing as eyewitnesses began to die off.

Where Do We Find the Real, Historical Jesus?

Many pseudo-scholarly professors, popular writers, and moviemakers want us to believe our best sources for the historical Jesus are not the books of Matthew, Mark, Luke, and John.

"The person these men portray is not the real Jesus," they say. "We've been fed all kinds of strange ideas, many of which have already been disproved."

Truthfully, much of this stuff is beyond belief. Some of these modern portraits of Jesus are based on the extracanonical gospels—again, books not in our Bibles—and invariably the Jesus that emerges is not the Christ of the Bible, not the Christ proclaimed by the apostles, and not the Christ of the faith of the early church. These extracanonical gospels are late, non-apostolic, and idiosyncratic, and they don't accurately depict the first-century world of Jesus. Novelist Dan Brown, the Jesus Seminar, hyperskeptical scholars, and others in their company have it all wrong because they use questionable sources. The Jesus Seminar's work is flawed because it leans heavily on some of these sources and measured the first-century New Testament Gospels in the light of these sources.

If you want the real Jesus, he can be found in first-century apostolic writings. If you're doing historical work, don't you want the earliest sources? If you're talking about somebody who said remarkable things and did astounding things, don't you want to hear from the people who saw him, knew him, and heard him? Without this help, it would be very difficult to talk about life 150 years ago. If you decided to write a journal pretending to be somebody who lived in the 1850s, you would probably make mistakes because you wouldn't be exactly sure how day-to-day living took place. You would slip up.

These extracanonical gospel writers slipped up many times. When the four Gospel writers of the Bible talked about the real Jesus in the AD 20s and 30s, they did not slip up.

Jesus' Resurrection as the Beginning

The Christian movement began with the proclamation of the resurrection of Jesus of Nazareth. Most skeptics regard the claim as unhistorical, yet most followers of Jesus (that is, Christians) believe he was in fact raised from the dead. Although it's disputed, most scholars believe that the resurrection of Jesus was understood as a bodily resurrection and not simply a spiritual resurrection. The point of Paul's argument in 1 Corinthians 15 was to affirm that the resurrection is bodily but not simply a reanimation.

The New Testament Gospels emphasize the bodily nature of the resurrection of Jesus. He could be touched (Luke 24:39; compare 1 John 1:1), his crucifixion wounds were visible (John 20:20, 24–28), and he ate food (Luke 24:41–43), which disembodied spirits cannot do. Moreover, the absence of Jesus' body from the tomb where he was buried (Luke 24:22–23) underscores the bodily nature of his resurrection. The bodily resurrection of Jesus, including prophecy that God's Holy One would not be abandoned to the grave, forms the basis of the early church's proclamation (Acts 2:22–36) and historic claim. The resurrection of Jesus became the central tenet of our Christian faith.

PART THREE

The 7 BEST REASONS to BELIEVE in the RESURRECTION of JESUS

4

Reason #1

*Society Is Transformed Everywhere Christianity
Is Introduced and Embraced*

More people attend church on Easter Sunday than watch the
Super Bowl. But what would our world be like if that first Easter
had never happened? If the Christian movement had never taken
off?

Good questions. But even speculatively guessing at an answer is a bit like the counter-factual narratives being told about
the resurrection today. For example, what if Greece had been
overwhelmed by Persia? What if Winston Churchill had given
up and Britain had surrendered? What if Hitler had won World
War II?

But we don't need to guess. We can study what the world
would be like without the resurrection of Jesus. And we already
have a pretty good idea of what the world was like before Jesus
and the Christian church (short answer: It was awful!). And
thanks to communism and Nazi Germany, we also have a pretty

good idea of what the world would become if Christianity were driven out of society.

Christianity has changed so much in the world. Christian belief is not indifferent to suffering. For instance, it successfully abolished slavery not once but twice—in late antiquity and again in the 1800s with the elimination of the transatlantic slave trade after the American Civil War. Much more could be said and has been written about the efforts of Christian leaders like William Wilberforce and John Wesley, who tirelessly worked in the eighteenth and nineteenth centuries to abolish slavery. (More recently, a third wave of Christians are at the forefront of ending slavery in the marginalized world.)

It should be noted that Wilberforce and Wesley lived during the so-called Age of Enlightenment. Were secular philosophers of the time "enlightened" to the evils of slavery? The simple answer is no. A Who's Who of major enlightenment figures supported slavery: Thomas Hobbes, John Locke, Voltaire, David Hume, and Edmund Burke, among others.

From only one religion or belief system historically emerged the conclusion that slavery was absolutely evil: Christianity. In contrast, Islam does not consider slavery to be a sin. Muhammad personally owned and sold slaves.[1] The Qur'an, Hadith, and Sira (Islamic trilogy) contain the most elaborate and comprehensive slave code in the world.[2] Islam has enslaved more people than any other culture and still practices slave owning in areas of Saudi Arabia, Mauritania, and Sudan.[3]

But the question *What would our modern world be like without Christianity and, specifically, the resurrection?* is a bit more foundational. Frankly, I'm not sure there would even be a modern world without it. To be sure, cultural and technological advances came about here and there. For one, the weapons of the Romans were more sophisticated than the weapons of the empires of the Ancient Near East. But Roman society was not much more advanced. Ideas of rights, law, and equality were nothing like what they would later become thanks to the emergence of Christianity.[4]

The impact of the Christian faith, of Jesus Christ himself on the world, is huge and probably impossible to measure fully. Every society where Christianity is introduced and embraced—from the first centuries AD to modern times—has been transformed, especially in the following four ways. As we will see, the church, unified and mobilized, is the greatest force for good on earth.

1. The Revelation of a Loving God

The revelation of a loving God was key to societal changes made in the first centuries AD—and still is today. In fact, one of the most startling and revolutionary teachings in the Christian message is that God loves humanity: "God so loved the world, that he gave his only Son" (John 3:16).

This idea rooted in the faith and Scriptures of ancient Israel would have struck first-century pagans as simply astounding. Some of their gods merely tolerated, while others did not tolerate, humankind. At best, they were indifferent to the human plight, and at worst, they resented humans and sometimes lusted after them. They toyed with them and often acted against them capriciously. That's why most pagans believed the gods felt little or no compassion for humans and some gods were even jealous of humans who were beautiful or gifted. They were petty, easily offended, and vengeful. Indeed, they were often deceitful and couldn't be trusted. Humans had to placate, cajole, and even bribe them.

Christianity's belief in one God changed all that. Christians not only proclaimed that "God is love" but that he sent his Son to bring reconciliation between God and humanity—to redeem them. Ancient pagans had never heard of such a thing. The God of Jesus, described as a heavenly Father who loved his children, who was patient with them when they were foolish and sinful, and who was a wholly reliable, faithful God of truth, was simply mind-boggling for them. Almost incomprehensible.

On top of that, this Son of God was raised up to a new and glorious life. Not only could humans be reconciled to God, but they could be assured of a new and perfect life in the world to come—something the people of the pagan world could only wish for, never knowing if it could be attained.

It's no surprise, then, that the Christian message of a loving, redeeming God has attracted 2.4 billion followers, more than any other faith. And as the gospel continues to be shared around the world, so may Christ's followers increase.

2. Improvement in Ethics and Morals

The Christian influence was such that by the end of the fourth century, when the Roman Empire itself, rife with corruption, was beginning to crumble, philosophies of racism disappeared. Cruelty, such as crucifixion and the gladiatorial games, came to an end. The treatment of women and children improved. And as time went on, no more intellectuals called for infanticide in the name of eugenics or economics. Slavery began to recede.

3. More Social and Cultural Freedoms for Women

The resurrection of Jesus was compelling in the early church, especially to women. The Jewish scriptures taught that God made humans in his image, and Jesus and his followers rightly inferred from this teaching that men and women are equal. They may have different, complementary roles in the family and in public, but in the eyes of God, they are equals.

Early Christians demonstrated this belief by entrusting positions of leadership to women. Gifted, educated women were permitted to speak in the Christian communities and churches and exercise that leadership. The church also showed compassion to the sick, poor, and homeless, and that compassion and mercy attracted women, who often felt abused and unloved.

4. Strides in Science, the Arts, and the Quality of Life

Modern science had its beginning. The moon and planets were assumed to follow a regular course. The very elements of the created order were assumed to make sense and were open to discovery. Since humankind was made in the image of God—an idea pagan antiquity thought absurd—it was assumed that humans should explore the beautiful world that God had made, that such exploration would in fact be successful, that there was much both beautiful and practical to be learned.

And so one discovery after another was made. The world was a sphere. Oceans could be crossed. Vast new continents and their riches could be discovered and explored. Technologies of every kind were invented and put to use. Barbarian Europe was transformed into the greatest, most technologically and educationally advanced society on the planet, leaping past the older near eastern and far eastern civilizations.

The Christian world expanded the arts—music, literature, visual art. Literacy was encouraged. It's not a coincidence that the greatest art, literature, and music focuses on Christian and biblical themes. *The Last Supper* painted by Leonardo da Vinci, the Sistine Chapel ceiling painted by Michelangelo, the endless paintings of the old masters . . . all were inspired by Jesus and the movement he launched. Architecture, too, was deeply influenced by Jesus and Christian theism. The spires of Oxford, the great cathedrals of continental Europe, and indeed, the very halls of government display the inspiration of the West's faith in God and its devotion to Jesus Christ, the Son of God.

The message that God loves humanity, that he is a God of truth and not of deceit and trickery, that the world he created is good and not capricious and chaotic, laid the foundation on which education could be built and compassion realized. Christianized Europe founded universities, schools, orphanages, hospitals, and one charity after another.

It's inconceivable that any of this would exist today if Jesus had not come and the church he founded had never happened. Would Europeans still be savages in the forest, fighting among themselves and attacking strangers who happened to pass by? What would have changed the near zero literacy rates of Europe had the message of Christ and Holy Scripture not entered this pagan world?

Would we have modern medicine today had the world not been transformed by Christ and his heavenly Father? I suspect that instead of doctors, we'd have only witch doctors and shamans. Instead of medicine and surgery, we'd have spells and magic. And what of modern education? Would it exist? I doubt it very much. Would we enjoy modern transportation? Or would we still be traveling on foot and on horse? Would we enjoy modern communication? Or would we be using smoke signals and pigeons instead of our smartphones and the internet?

What Makes Christianity Unique?

Most of the pre-Christian world was polytheistic, but thanks to Jesus and his movement, a majority of the world now believes in one God (one-third of the world's population follows Jesus). Moreover, most of the world believes Jesus was a significant person even if many don't believe in him in the way Christians do. Consequently, to some extent many of his teachings are heeded and the world has been Christianized. Again, this has resulted in an enormous improvement in the quality of life.

Christianity is also the only faith that holds the view that God himself has purchased our redemption. In no other religious thought or system do we find God or any god who suffers for humanity and in doing so brings about redemption. All other systems teach either that we learn to accept life as it is or we attempt to redeem ourselves.

Why some people respond to God's loving grace and find redemption and others don't is difficult to determine. Hitler had a moment when a priest challenged him to abandon his evil, violent past. He was initially shaken but then chose to ignore the pastoral warning. Hitler hardened his heart, even as Pharaoh did thousands of years ago, and then led Germany on a path that resulted in unimaginable death and destruction.

Hitler did not believe in God in any conventional sense. The enlightenment-driven atheism of the twentieth century served Hitler well, because without God, he could easily do away with the Judeo-Christian worldview and the ethics and morals that went with it. With God out of the picture, it was easier to argue for the elimination of unwanted people, easier to justify violence, easier to justify war, easier to promote a superior race or ideology that trampled people underfoot. In short, if you want to be a thug, it's a lot easier without God muddying the waters.

Despite men like Hitler, though, there's no doubt that our modern world would be radically different without Easter. Without the emergence of Christianity, the pagan world would have continued. Nothing much would have changed it.

And that world was hell on earth.

5

Reason #2

Jesus Called It—#OnTheThirdDay

At Wrigley Field on October 1, 1932, with two balls and two strikes at the top of the fifth inning, "The Babe" called his shot. With Lou Gehrig on deck, Babe Ruth crushed Charlie Root's pitch deep into the center-field seats for a monstrous home run in the face of merciless Cubs fans and the trash-talking Cubs bench. The Bambino's called shot broke a 4–4 tie with the Cubs and powered the Yankees to victory in game 3 and eventually the Fall Classic.

Sports reporter Joe Williams, covering the World Series for the *New York World-Telegram*, coined the phrase "called shot." Otherwise, what happened may have been lost to history. The headline ran RUTH CALLS SHOT AS HE PUTS HOME RUN NO. 2 IN SIDE POCKET. Even so, there's been some debate about whether Ruth was only pointing or if he really did call his shot. Eighty-eight years later, Lou Gehrig biographer Dan Joseph unearthed a Gehrig radio interview from October 6 of that year, and in it Lou set the record straight:

He stands up there and tells the world that he's going to sock that next one. And not only that, but he tells the world right where he's going to sock it, into the center-field stands. A few seconds later, the ball was just where he pointed, in the center-field stands. He called his shot and then made it. I ask you: What can you do with a guy like that?[1]

Predictions are fascinating, and when they come true, they're compelling. Skeptics wonder if Jesus knew what he was doing. Yes, Jesus knew exactly what he was doing. Indeed, he called his shot too.

What Explains the Growth of the Early Christian Movement?

As I wrote in *Unanswered*,

> If I were a critic of Christianity, perhaps the most difficult problem would be coming up with a reason for why there are any Christians . . . in the first place. Their founder was a crucified criminal. Crucifixion was considered to be the most heinous and shameful way to die. In the gospel of Luke, His disciples are said to have lost all hope following the crucifixion. They gave up, and why would they not? In that gripping scene in Luke 24:13–35, two disciples on the Emmaus road encounter an interesting stranger. Not realizing they are walking and conversing with the resurrected Messiah, they admitted, "We had hoped that he was the one" (Luke 24:21). The early Christian movement should have died out, but instead it thrived. Why? The resurrection of Jesus.[2]

Fascinatingly, Jesus wasn't the only individual claiming to be the Messiah in the first century, nor in the second century. Specific individuals saw themselves as "Israel's Savior" insofar as they desired to rule all Israel, cleanse a corrupt priesthood, vanquish the Roman occupiers, and restore Jewish culture. There were at least ten "messianic pretenders" or claimants in addition to Jesus of Nazareth. These included Judah, Simon, Athronges following the death of Herod the Great in 4 BC, and Menahem and Simon bar Giora during the Jewish revolt of AD 66–70.

Additional Messianic Pretenders

- *The Anonymous Samaritan* (AD 26–36). According to the first-century historian Josephus, during the administration of Pontius Pilate, a certain Samaritan, whom he calls a liar and demagogue, convinced many of his people to follow him to Mount Gerizim, where he would show them the place where their sacred temple vessels were buried.
- *Theudas* (AD 44–46). Luke tells us about Theudas in Acts 5:36: "Some time ago Theudas appeared, claiming to be somebody, and about four hundred men rallied to him. He was killed, all his followers were dispersed, and it all came to nothing" (NIV).
- *The Anonymous Egyptian* (AD 56). Luke also mentions this imposter: "Aren't you the Egyptian who started a revolt and led four thousand terrorists out into the wilderness some time ago?" (Acts 21:38 NIV).
- *Jesus son of Ananias* (AD 62–69). Josephus tells us this Jesus proclaimed the doom of the temple and city. His strange oracle appeared to be based on Jeremiah 7:34.[3]
- *Jonathan the refugee* (AD 70–79). Also according to Josephus, this man persuaded many of the poorer Jews to follow him out into the desert, "promising to show them signs and apparitions."[4]

The Importance of Jesus' Passion and Resurrection Promises

If the early church had had a hashtag, it would have been #onthe thirdday. These words were critical for the earliest witnesses of the resurrection. They were the most important words in Christian origins and in the early church (Acts 10:40; 1 Corinthians

15:4). In the eighth century BC, the Israelite prophet Hosea had used those words to console a defeated Northern Kingdom with the promise that God would restore the nation. Then anticipating the eventual restoration of sinful Israel, he uttered a startling prediction: "After two days he will revive us; on the third day he will raise us up, that we may live before him" (Hosea 6:2).

This is one of the most important Bible texts for understanding the interpretation and self-understanding of Jesus, because it lies behind his passion predictions. As I've written in yet another book,

> We hear [Hosea's] prophecy echoed in Jesus' predictions of suffering: "The Son of Man will be delivered into the hands of men, and they will kill him; and when he is killed, after three days he will rise" (Mark 9:31; compare Mark 8:31; 10:33–34). Indeed, the resurrected Jesus himself alludes to Hosea's prophecy: "Thus it is written, that the Christ should suffer and on the third day rise from the dead" (Luke 24:46).[5]

As I noted, the prophet Hosea originally spoke of national restoration, a time not too far off in the future, when God would restore the wayward Northern Kingdom. As noted previously, it was in later traditions that Hosea 6:2 came to be understood as in reference to resurrection, but it was always understood to be in reference to the general resurrection of the final judgment. What appears to be Jesus' unique contribution is applying the prophecy to himself, to a single individual, probably implying his resurrection before the general resurrection.

Jesus' passion predictions, even if edited and contextualized by the Gospel evangelists, likely preserve an authentic core. At the heart of this core lie two principal components: (1) In Jerusalem Jesus would suffer and die, and (2) "after three days" or "on the third day," Jesus would be raised up.[6]

Jesus Predicts His Violent Death

"He began to teach them that the Son of Man must suffer many things and be rejected by the elders and the chief priests and the scribes and be killed, and after three days rise again" (Mark 8:31).

"The Son of man will be delivered into the hands of men, and they will kill him; and when he is killed, after three days he will rise" (Mark 9:31 RSV).

"Behold, we are going up to Jerusalem; and the Son of man will be delivered to the chief priests and scribes, and they will condemn him to death, and deliver him to the Gentiles; and they will mock him, and spit upon him, and scourge him, and kill him; and after three days he will rise" (Mark 10:33–34 RSV).

Matthew, Mark, and Luke (the Synoptic Gospels) significantly emphasize Jesus' passion predictions using "on the third day" or "after three days" again and again. It's fascinating that Jesus "messianizes" Hosea 6:1–3, which means he applies these passages to himself. You can read the three biggies above (Mark 8:31, Mark 9:31, Mark 10:33–34), but that review is representative, not exhaustive. The risen Jesus teaches more than once from Hosea in discussion with the disciples on the road to Emmaus (Luke 24:13–27) and during another appearance (24:44–49: "It is written, that the Christ should suffer and on the third day rise from the dead" [verse 46]).[7]

Predictions and Expectations

Jesus predicted his death and resurrection on more than one occasion, and those predictions provided his followers with the foundation for understanding what was to take place. Without them, the disciples would have been left wondering about the whole point of his ministry.

Judas Iscariot never saw the resurrected Christ. He probably decided to quit following Jesus and give up because he was disillusioned. Like many of his contemporaries, he probably hoped for a conqueror. He didn't understand Jesus' kingdom message and ministry.

Throughout the Gospels, we see that the disciples struggled to understand the true purpose of Jesus' ministry. They expected the Romans to be driven out of Israel; a corrupt, abusive high priesthood to be overthrown; and Jerusalem to be purged. These were messianic expectations many Jews held to. The Messiah would be a conqueror, he would vanquish the Jews' enemies, and he would restore Jerusalem to its former glory.

Judas's decision to betray Jesus was confirmed when a woman anointed Jesus in the Bethany home of Simon the leper, pouring an expensive ointment over Jesus' head. Instead of responding, "Yes, this is my messianic anointing. Yes, with God's help we will overthrow the Romans," he said, "She has anointed my body beforehand for burial" (Mark 14:8). For Judas, this was the last straw (verse 10). This event also greatly influenced the rest of the disciples, so Jesus knew he must instruct them. That's the point of his words at the Last Supper: "Take it; this is my body. . . . This is my blood of the covenant, which is poured out for many" (Mark 14:22–24 NIV).

Few of Jesus' words are as familiar as those he uttered at the Last Supper. According to the tradition passed down to the apostle Paul, Jesus then added, "Do this in remembrance of me" (1 Corinthians 11:24–25 NIV). This statement clearly alludes to Exodus 24:8: "This is the blood of the covenant that the LORD has made with you in accordance with all these words."

The new covenant, which would have been recognized by Jesus and his contemporaries, is the promise of Jeremiah 31:31: "Behold, the days are coming, declares the LORD, when I will make a new covenant with the house of Israel and the house of Judah." Jesus was predicting and heralding a new covenant that would be related to the Sinai covenant of shed blood, when Moses said, "This is the blood of the covenant" (Exodus 24:8 NIV). Jesus took the two Old Testament covenants and merged them together in his own death and resurrection.

He would be that sacrifice. Atonement would not be through the blood of bulls and goats but through his own blood.

A Proclamation of Jesus' Continuing Ministry

Jesus' words at the Last Supper laid the groundwork so that when the disciples were stunned by the empty tomb and the resurrection appearances a few days later, they would be able to look back and understand that Jesus' death was not a disruption; rather, it furthered the kingdom proclamation. What we call the Words of Institution (Matthew 26:26–29; Mark 14:22–25; Luke 22:14–20) redefined and reempowered their mission, their proclamation, of a Messiah who in fact would save them.

But not by killing Romans. Instead, Jesus' death and resurrection defeated the ultimate enemies of all humans: sin and death. Jesus' words provided his disciples (and all Christians) with the theological context for understanding the significance of the resurrection. Again, without Jesus' passion predictions, the disciples would have been very confused about the point of his ministry. His death and resurrection were seen as a consummation of God's saving work, his redeeming work for all humanity. Indeed, they were a proclamation of his continuing ministry to advance the kingdom of God but now clearly focused on the redemption of the entire world.

The risen Jesus told his disciples to go out and make disciples of the nations and all peoples. The commission was not limited to Israel: "You shall receive power when the Holy Spirit has come upon you; and you shall be my witnesses both in Jerusalem and in all Judea and Samaria and to the end of the earth"

(Acts 1:8 RSV). It was Israel's story, but as the promises to the prophets and patriarchs hinted at, it was to be life-changing for the entire world, not simply the exaltation of a single people at the expense of Gentile neighbors. It would be a redeeming, restorative, redemptive ministry that would affect the entire planet and, in the end, reverse and cure the negative consequence of humankind's sin and fall.

Christians partake in the Lord's Supper to remember and proclaim Jesus' death until he comes again (1 Corinthians 11:26), but they also reflect on his resurrection, proclaiming the fact that he lives.

Jesus brought the Lord's Supper in the upper room to a conclusion with these words: "I tell you, I will not drink from this fruit of the vine from now on until that day when I drink it new with you in my Father's kingdom" (Matthew 26:29 NIV).

The Lord's Day

Not only did Jesus rise on Sunday, but six of his post-resurrection appearances also took place on Sunday. The day of Pentecost—when the body of Christ, the church, was formed—also fell on Sunday. Almost always in the Bible, Sunday is designated as the first day of the week (Matthew 28:1; Mark 16:2, 9; Luke 24:1). In Revelation 1:10 it's called the Lord's day, a term similar to the Lord's supper (1 Corinthians 11:20) and used by the believers to protest and contrast the Emperor's Day (or Augustus's Day). The term *Lord's Day*, then, is the first day of the week, remembering the day of Jesus' resurrection.

Another important resurrection tradition linked with "the third day" dominical tradition (meaning it's related to Jesus as Lord or the Lord's Day) and also unique to early Christian texts was a new day of communal worship. The day of worship for Christians migrated from the Jewish Sabbath to Sunday, resurrection day ("the third day"), as a continuing testimony of the church to the centrality of the resurrection (Acts 20:7; 1 Corinthians 16:2).

Therefore, Jesus not only discussed and predicted his imminent resurrection but also commanded his disciples, whom he sent out as apostles, to proclaim the kingdom of God and to "raise the dead" (Matthew 10:8). These mighty works foreshadowed the resurrection anticipated at the end of days. The resurrection of Jesus on the third day threw the message of the kingdom of God into a new light.

For the Christian, resurrection isn't celebrated on Easter alone but on every Lord's Day. The phrase *the first day of the week* was not found in Jewish tradition until the Gospel writers used it (see for example Matthew 28:1). Think about how important the gathering of the local church was to the first Christians. Should it not be the same for us today? Every time we gather on the first day of the week, we give testimony to Jesus' resurrection.[8]

6

Reason #3

Jesus Demonstrated Resurrection Power

Jesus' belief in resurrection can be observed in the canonical Gospels via the miracles he performs by resuscitation. They are related eschatological examples of the final defeat of death. Resuscitations were an aspect of Jesus' ministry of raising up the "recently deceased" that foreshadowed the future resurrections on the day of judgment as an eschatological event.

I also shared this in my book *Unanswered*, but it bears repeating:

> Jesus authorized his disciples to preach the good news of the reign of God and, among other things, to "raise the dead" (Matthew 10:8). In his reply to the imprisoned John, Jesus says, "The dead are raised up" (Matthew 11:5; Luke 7:22). In addition to these summary statements, the New Testament Gospels narrate three specific stories of people raised from the dead by Jesus.
>
> In one story, Jesus raises the daughter of Jairus, the ruler of a synagogue, whose daughter had died only moments before Jesus

arrived (Mark 5:21–43; Matthew 9:18–26; Luke 8:40–56). The story's details may suggest firsthand eyewitness testimony—from the desperation of the father and the sad report that reached him ("Your daughter is dead. Why trouble the Teacher any further?" [Mark 5:35]) to the mocking laughter in response to Jesus' words ("Why do you make a tumult and weep? The child is not dead but sleeping" [verse 39 RSV]). The very Aramaic words Jesus uttered remained fixed in the tradition: *talitha, cum* ("Little girl, arise"). The appearance of the name Jairus, along with his identification with respect to the local synagogue (probably the one at Capernaum), probably points to the memory of a specific episode in the ministry of Jesus.

In the second story, Jesus raises up the only son of a widow (Luke 7:11–17). He encounters the funeral party as it leaves the village of Nain on its way to the place of burial. The boy has died that very day or perhaps the previous evening. A number of distinctive details are recalled, such as the name of the village, the woman being a widow, the deceased boy her only son, Jesus' touching the bier, the stopping of the bearers, and the startling movement of the deceased, who is said to have "sat up." Again we have vivid details that probably derive from eyewitness memory.

The third resuscitation story is the well-known raising of Lazarus, arguably the most stunning miracle story in the Jesus tradition. Lazarus was the brother of Mary and Martha, part of a family that lived in Bethany, in the vicinity of Jerusalem (John 11:1–44). We're told that Lazarus had been ill, had finally died, and that four days after his death Jesus finally arrived.

The raising of Lazarus is by far the most dramatic resuscitation story in the Gospels. In contrast to the others who died and then minutes or at most hours later were raised up, Lazarus has been dead for four days. He's been wrapped and placed in the family tomb. The seven-day primary funeral, held at the graveside, is more than half completed. Then Jesus arrives, requests that the stone be removed, and is told that there will be a stench (11:39).

According to Jewish traditions, the spirit of the deceased lingers in the vicinity of the corpse for three days and then departs on the fourth day. From the Jewish perspective of late antiquity, Lazarus is as dead as one can get. Nothing less than "resurrection," in its eschatological sense, can bring him back. His sisters believe this; but as far as this life is concerned, they will never see their brother again. Jesus then commands, "Lazarus, come forth," and then "the man who had died came out bound hand and foot with wrappings" (verses 43–44 NASB). The story is remarkable.

In all three of these stories, we find what appear to be traces of eyewitness memory, the recollection of names, places, unusual and vivid details, and even some of Jesus' words. Twice we hear him command the deceased: "Arise," either in Greek, as in Luke 7:14, or in Aramaic, as in Mark 5:41. The distinctive words of Jesus are remembered in whatever language they happen to be transmitted.

What's interesting is that in all three examples, specific details are retained: in the first story the name and position of Jairus, in the second story the name of the village and the facts that the woman was a widow and the dead boy was her only son, and in the third story the names of the deceased and his sisters, as well as how long he had been dead and the name of their village. Clearly many details, as well as the resuscitations themselves, were firmly embedded in the collective memory of Jesus' following.

I emphasize these remarkable stories because it's probable that they influenced the way the followers of Jesus interpreted the Easter event. From our point of view, privileged with hindsight, we may view these miraculous resuscitations as a harbinger of the resurrection of Jesus and of the future resurrection of his followers. But from the point of view of those who encountered the risen Jesus, with no well-established, uniform doctrine of resurrection before them, the miraculous resuscitations very probably defined aspects of Jesus' resurrection. I don't see how it could have been otherwise. Perhaps it's not coincidence that the same language is used in reference to those Jesus raised up, as well as in reference to his own resurrection.[1]

Clarifying Resurrection versus Resuscitation

In my scholarship, I've reviewed dozens of books related to the topic of resurrection, the immortality of the soul, and life after death. One of the confusing aspects of such a survey is that terms relating to life after death aren't used consistently, and even more confusing, a word can mean different things to different audiences. For example, returning from the dead has been described in literature as rebirth, resuscitation, reanimation, revivification, and of course, resurrection.

This lack of clarity also impacts our understanding of not only Jesus' resurrection but our own eventual resurrection. Let me be biblically clear with regard to Jesus' resurrection: Jesus was not resuscitated, reanimated, rebirthed, or revived. When scholars discuss Jesus as bodily resurrected, we describe a physical body that returns back to life from the dead, never to die again. The resurrected body is *un-dieable*, a term I've created for this book!

However, for interpretive precision, I incorporate the term *resuscitation* (not *resurrection*) where I interpret those who were miraculously brought back from death before Jesus' resurrection in the New Testament. Resuscitation involves a miracle where a person is brought back to life from the dead but will experience death again (or die twice, to say it another way).

It's not completely clear how, in the world of late antiquity, individuals would have differentiated resurrection versus resuscitation wording. The original Greek New Testament texts don't differentiate but use only resurrection vocabulary. The crowd gathered with Jesus, having experienced the decay and stench of Lazarus's death, saw him raised, walking, talking, and eating in their midst (John 11:1–44; 12:1–2). I'm not sure that, in the moment of this miracle, they would even have a category or descriptor. Abandonment from the grave was normally described by two Greek words in the New Testament that meant "to stand up" and "to rise, to have risen," but the authors usually didn't differentiate as to the circumstances of the resurrection.[2]

No Jew in the first century would have expected or anticipated an individual body returning to life following death. In fact, their only resurrection expectation was a general resurrection of the Jewish people of God at the end of time. In the excerpt from my book *Unanswered* earlier in this chapter, I reviewed Jesus' resurrection power and discussed the miraculous resuscitations, such as that of the widow of Nain's son, which in the Jewish mindset of the time could point to the general resurrection as an example. But it was only that—an example, because her son would die again. As such, interpretively we understand that Lazarus would die a second time. And Jairus's daughter would eventually die again. I expect they were not too afraid to die a second time in light of the experience of Jesus and his power over death.

One of the go-to texts regarding Jesus' altogether unique, distinctive, and *un-dieable* resurrected body is Revelation 1:18: "I died, and behold I am alive forevermore." Jesus' body will never die again. I love how Dr. Luke explicitly states that those who are resurrected "cannot die anymore" (Luke 20:36). In fact, our resurrected bodies will be intricately upgraded in that they will live on, no longer subject to disease, decay, and death. Our decaying bodies, rotting from sin, will be transformed into glorified bodies on which death can make no impact.

Further, as followers did in the first century, we struggle to describe our Marvel-esque resurrection bodies' otherworldly qualities not inherent in mortal bodies or resuscitated ones, such as the ability to appear and disappear from sight immediately: "He vanished from their sight" (Luke 24:31). Or to appear inside a closed room: "On the evening of that day, the first day of the week, the doors being shut where the disciples were, for fear of the Jews, Jesus came and stood among them and said to them, 'Peace be with you'" (John 20:19 RSV).

Further Clarifying Resurrection versus Resuscitation

As I mentioned earlier, abandonment from the grave was normally described by two Greek words in the New Testament. But the authors usually didn't differentiate as to the circumstances of the resurrection of the body coming back to life (would it die again or be "un-dieable"?). Those two words are ἀνάστασις (literally, "to stand up") and ἐγείρω ("to rise, to have risen").

For the pastors, Bible study teachers, educators, parents, and Christian thinkers who are studying this book, I want to give guidance with excellent interpretive (exegetical) techniques by way of the biblical texts.

My (now) dear friend, Professor Paul Foster (University of Edinburgh), who earned a DPhil from Oxford, trained me in exegetical methods. And he introduced me to, dare I say, "trendy" methods that allow the Bible student to offer more precision to the exegetical payoff of the text. These trendy insights are called "emic" and "etic" categories.

In the section above, I distinguished language in a way the ancient world would not have been familiar with. In other words, some of the terms commonly used aren't implicitly found in the text. As we do research and learn history, scholars (and Bible students and teachers, for that matter), clarify biblical concepts in a more distinctive way by using emic and etic categories of terms in our critical insights.

An emic category of interpretation is words or terms we can read in the original biblical text. They were real in the world of the people (for example, the word *resurrection*).

An etic category means the term isn't used in the ancient nomenclature. For example, we apply the word *resuscitation* to those who were miraculously brought back to life but would die again in the future.

In the previous section, I used etic terminology to create a distinction between two types of experiences in rising from the dead (a resurrected body that cannot die again versus a body that will die a second time). I had in view someone who was dead for a meaningful amount of time, such as the widow of Nain's son, or Lazarus, or the daughter of Jairus. By divine intervention, they were brought back to life. They were not, however, brought back to everlasting life.

Two more examples are helpful as we become better Bible exegetes.

In the Gospels, we find a term that's an emic category—*parousia*. We find it in the world of the text παρουσία, a Greek Word meaning "presence" or "coming." In the New Testament, it's almost always used in reference to Jesus' second coming. Parousia is real or inside the world of the people I'm describing.

An etic category might be the Trinitarian theology of Matthew's Gospel. Matthew never uses the word *trinity*. In fact, the Latin *trinitas* originated with Tertullian, the early church father. The New Testament authors didn't use the term *trinity* or have that concept. I have brought the concept to the text to try to clarify something.

Therefore, these emic and etic critical insights and distinctions (*resuscitation* compared with *resurrection*) allow precision to be brought to the examination of afterlife beliefs within the world of the New Testament and help us in our own understanding of Jesus' resurrection and our own eventual bodily resurrection.

Resurrection Beliefs Were Embraced in Early Judaism

Some wrongly think only pious people or eccentrics of Jesus' day believed in bodily resurrection, but even Jewish skeptics believed in resurrection. Herod Antipas, for instance, was well informed about Jesus and asked if he was the beheaded John the Baptist raised from the dead (Mark 6:16; Matthew 14:1–12; compare Luke 9:7–9).[3]

The backstory is interesting. John the Baptist publicly criti-cized Herod Antipas for taking his—Herod's—brother's wife in marriage, which set in motion a chain of events that led to Herod Antipas's imprisoning and eventually executing the Baptizer (Mark 6:17–29). Verses 14–16 lead us to understand Herod was haunted by a guilty conscience after the execution. People in Palestine were comparing Jesus' miraculous works with a vindicated and resuscitated martyr, John the Baptist: "Now Herod the tetrarch heard about all that was happen-ing, and he was perplexed, because it was said by some that John had been raised from the dead, by some that Elijah had appeared, and by others that one of the prophets of old had risen" (Luke 9:7–8).

This interesting story, recorded in the Synoptic Gospels (Matthew, Mark, and Luke) suggests resurrection beliefs were widespread in the first-century Jewish world.

Another example is the apostle Paul's letter to the church at Corinth, which the majority of scholars believe is, chronologi-cally, the earliest written Christian source for Jesus' resurrec-tion. It states, "As in Adam all die, so also in Christ shall all be made alive. But each in his own order: Christ the firstfruits, then at his coming those who belong to Christ. Then comes the end, when he delivers the kingdom to God the Father after destroying every rule and every authority and power" (1 Co-rinthians 15:22–24).

What's important about Paul's remarkable confession is the revelation that resurrection isn't innovative; rather, it rests on a firm foundation of early Christian preaching, early eyewitness testimony, creeds, and scriptural testimony.

As followers of Jesus, we live by faith in the tension between two resurrections: Jesus' first resurrection and our eventual own resurrection. The bodily resurrection of Jesus guarantees our future bodily resurrection. They are linked: "Christ has indeed been raised from the dead, the firstfruits of those who have fallen asleep" (1 Corinthians 15:20 NIV). We're also told that "our citizenship is in heaven. And we eagerly await a Savior from there, the Lord Jesus Christ, who, by the power that enables him to bring everything under his control, will transform our lowly bodies so that they will be like his glorious body" (Philippians 3:20–21 NIV).

Thanks to the resurrection of Jesus, Christians are promised that the best is yet to come, that death is only the beginning, not the end. That's why the apostle Paul told the Thessalonian Christians who had lost their loved ones that, though we grieve, we don't grieve like those who have no hope. That's because we know it's only a short interlude before we see them again (1 Thessalonians 4:13). The promise of 1 Corinthians 15 is that our deceased loved ones have not died in vain (verses 16–18).

But there's more. In the same passage in 1 Thessalonians, Paul answers at least four vital questions that give us hope now and in the future.

1. What Will the Resurrection Be Like at Jesus' Second Coming?

In 1 Corinthians 15:51–52, we're told that cosmic signs and miracles will hasten the resurrection of the dead. At the second coming of Christ, the dead will rise suddenly, and loud noises will accompany this apocalyptic hastening of the dead. In 1 Thessalonians, Paul states that three different sounds will be heard at the resurrection: the "cry of command" from "the Lord himself," "the voice of an archangel," and "the trumpet of God" (4:16).

2. What Kind of Resurrection Body Can We Expect?

Deathlessness is the main descriptor of our resurrection bodies. They cannot die. They will be literal, physical bodies, not spirit-ghosts or apparitions. We know this because Paul tells the church at Philippi that Christ will "transform our lowly body to be like his glorious body" (Philippians 3:21). Christ was raised in a physical body, and Scripture tells us our resurrection bodies will be patterned after his own body. Jesus also tells his disciples, "See my hands and my feet, that it is I myself. Touch me, and see. For a spirit does not have flesh and bones as you see that I have" (Luke 24:39).

3. Are Resurrection and Valuing Life Linked?

A belief in the resurrection also drove Christians to value all life, which included caring for the body in burial (which I discuss at greater length in the chapter on reason #7).

Paul used two descriptive words to characterize resurrection life in 1 Corinthians 15:53 (NIV): *imperishable* (a body that never needs to be upgraded) and *immortality* (a body that will never die). Paul's clear description of the resurrected state underscores why he expressed his desire to be with Jesus: "To me, to live is Christ and to die is gain" (Philippians 1:21 NIV).

It's difficult to watch our bodies break down. Are you feeling a little sore today? Is your body weaker than it once was? Are you having more "senior moments"? Are you fighting a disease? Our resurrection bodies will be "raised in glory . . . raised in power" (1 Corinthians 15:43 NIV). As believers, we know death is not the end. That doesn't mean we look forward to death, but as Pastor Greg Laurie has said that only those who are prepared to die are really ready to live.

4. Why Does the Resurrection Matter for Us Today?

Paul concluded this teaching with a powerful point in verse 58: What happens in the future with your resurrection body affects everything you do for God today. That's why Paul used the present tense, "Your labor in the Lord is not in vain" (NIV), rather than the future tense, "Your labor will not be in vain." He was challenging believers to never give up, to never quit, but instead to "be steadfast, immovable, always excelling in the Lord's work" (HCSB). The resurrection not only shapes our future but energizes our present ministry for the kingdom of God. We should never lack motivation to serve God with all our heart, because we know everything we do for him will last for all eternity. Any suffering we endure for Jesus' sake will be worth it when we see him and are welcomed into his eternal kingdom.

Christians can be as solid as a rock—steadfast and immovable—because since the worst enemy, death, is defeated, we have nothing to fear. We need to be strong. The resurrection promises us that our lives have eternal significance when devoted to our ever-living, resurrected Lord.

As I close this chapter, think about what it would have been like to be among the eleven disciples proceeding up the mount of Jesus' ascension in Matthew 28. The text says, "When they saw Him, they worshiped Him; but some were doubtful" (verse 17 NASB).

The word *doubt* or *doubtful* in that verse (*distazo* in the Greek) means to waver, hesitate, and lack confidence. Where are you today on the mount of ascension? Are you worshiping, or are you doubtful? Or both? How did Jesus respond when some worshiped and others doubted? He told them, "Go therefore and make disciples of all the nations" (Matthew 28:19 NASB). Jesus met his followers right where they were—some worshiping and others doubting—and put them on a mission.

You can be used by God and actively serve him while negotiating the doubts in your faith. Doubts don't sideline you. Some days you're on the mountain, seeing the resurrected Jesus and worshiping him, and other days you find yourself doubting. But God still has a plan for you—to go and be used. He will be with you, as Jesus promised.

Jesus' fame as a miracle worker, a healer, and one who could raise the dead—indeed, one who had power over death—foreshadowed his own future resurrection. Our reasons #2 and #3 build on each other. Jesus not only predicted his future death and resurrection but proved he had power over death by miraculously bringing others back from death.

7

Reason #4

No Motivation to Invent Jesus'
Resurrection Narrative Is Evident

The case for the resurrection of Jesus falls under two broad headings: (1) the lack of a coherent and compelling alternative explanation, and (2) substantial direct and circumstantial evidence in support of the resurrection. We've already reviewed the lack of a coherent and compelling alternative explanation, and the balance of our discussion will focus on the evidence suggesting that Jesus may well have been raised from the dead.

As far as I can tell, this fourth reason—that no psychological motivation to invent the story of Jesus' resurrection narrative is evident—represents an original and fresh argument in favor of Jesus' resurrection. It's easy to anachronistically read our modern understanding of Jesus' vindication over death back into the world of Jesus and his first followers. If, however, you'd been alive in the time of Jesus, you would know his bodily resurrection was *not* what his disciples (or any other Jews, for that matter) anticipated. What is the psychological motivation to invent a story of Jesus' resurrection if you already believe in the general resurrection at the end of time? There is none.

In one of the most striking scenes in the Gospel narratives, Jesus replies to Peter, "Get behind me, Satan!" (Matthew 16:23). Why was Jesus so direct with Peter? Immediately following another prediction of Jesus' violent death and resurrection and just before Jesus said this to Peter, Peter "took him aside and began to rebuke him, saying, 'Far be it from you, Lord! This shall never happen to you'" (verse 22). Mark's earlier account even details the clarity of Jesus' dying and rising predictions: "And [Jesus] said this plainly" (Mark 8:32).

Peter still didn't understand, and he usually spoke for the disciples as a group. Therefore, we see clearly that none of the disciples understood that Jesus' messianic mission included death and resurrection. Peter aggressively tried to stop Jesus from discussing dying, which helps us understand the strength of Jesus' counter-rebuke of Peter.

It's so important that we don't miss the fact that Jesus' disciples had no earthly motivation to invent a resurrection story on behalf of Jesus the Messiah. And, again, I'm not sure anyone has talked about that in the discussion of the resurrection of Jesus. So let us suppose that Jesus dies on the cross and is buried but for the moment leave open the question of the resurrection. Why would Jesus' followers make up the resurrection if there was no certainty of it—none at all? The New Testament says he was resurrected. His earliest followers believed he was resurrected.

In fact, maybe there was certainty that he was *not* resurrected. His body was someplace, so why would anyone be motivated to make up an extraordinary, grotesque story about a risen Jesus? (And by the way, the early Greeks found it grotesque. Critics in the second and third centuries—Celsus, Porphyry, and others— reacted with horror at the idea of a bodily resurrection. See the chapter 3 discussion about objectors.)

Resurrection is not an obvious or winning proclamation for them. In fact, it's not obvious that the proclamation about the resurrection of a dead body will serve the interests of their community and help it grow and expand.

And why would Jews be motivated to do that, anyway? They had plenty of martyr stories. Numerous martyrs had died, and the Jewish people believed their spirits lived on in the presence of God. In other words, they died, but they went to heaven. These beliefs were embraced by later rabbis, people who had lived prior to the time of Christianity, the Pharisees, and of course, Jesus' own followers. To be clear, they believed you didn't need a resurrection story in order for a loved one to be spiritually in the presence of God.

Another important psychological perspective comes into play: You don't need to create a new religion either. If you're Jewish, if you're a devout, Torah-observant Jew, you believe that Israel has a covenant with God thanks to Mount Sinai and Moses. The covenant includes the laws of Moses, you have the prophets, and you have these exhortations about how to live pious lives. The Jewish prophetic scriptures promise someday God will redeem Israel. You also have a hope of afterlife if you choose to have it, and many Jews did, notably the Pharisees and others.

So here's the question: Why do you need to invent something new—a new religion? If Jesus talked about being resurrected, but they killed him and he stayed dead in his tomb, what would motivate you to make up a resurrection story?

If you're Jewish, you don't need it!

Again, you have prophecies that someday God will redeem Israel. You have a hope of an afterlife. You already have a coherent religious system. You can still identify your tradition, your legacy, your heritage in distinction from the Greco-Roman one, which is polytheistic—and from your point of view, morally reprobate. In late Second Temple Judaism, you have cohesion, you have community, you have legacy, you have a future, and the last thing you need is a charlatan, false messiah. The last thing you need is a goofy story about someone resurrected for which there isn't any evidence.

Therefore, a burden of proof rests heavily upon the Christians for themselves, not just in making the case to skeptics. You could say, "I'm a loyal Jesus follower, and I think everything he taught is true. I'm crushed and grief-stricken he's dead, but I still believe in him. I believe he's in heaven, and I believe he will be vindicated gloriously someday in judgment. He's right now at God's right-hand side, and I will continue to believe that."

You could say all that without one word about resurrection. You could believe in the resurrection someday in the future as pious Jews did, as Pharisees did. You don't have to have Jesus resurrected if there simply isn't any evidence that he was resurrected. It isn't required.

Let's be clear: No emotional pressure, no intellectual drive, and no doctrinaire commitment makes you say, "Jesus has to be resurrected or I simply cannot go on living" or "Jesus has to be resurrected or I'll face an emotional and psychological crisis." There's no reason for that at all.

In the first-century world, you could proclaim, "I'm Jewish. I believe in God and I believe in future resurrection. I believe in justice someday, vindication, and I can continue to cling to that hope. I can even believe Jesus was right and was a great man and was a prophet, and maybe even God's Son despite what happened to him. And I don't need to create a make-believe unhistorical lie and tell everybody he was resurrected when in fact he wasn't."

The burden of proof rests heavily on proof that he really was resurrected.

The Followers' Attitudes and Motivations

Several lines of evidence, everywhere reflected in the writings that make up the New Testament, support the early Christian belief that Jesus was in fact raised from the dead. The first line of evidence asks why, after his crucifixion, his followers spoke of him as the Messiah and the Son of God, the true redeemer of Israel.

Surely his death on a Roman cross—viewed as shameful and disgraceful—would have disqualified Jesus. Why would any of his followers have regarded their master—no matter how great a teacher he might have been—as Israel's Messiah? After all, it was widely believed that the Messiah would defeat the Romans, drive them from the land, and lead Israel to unprecedented heights of glory. Yet Jesus did none of that. He died, he was buried, and his family and disciples mourned.

What, then, can account for the sudden change of attitude among the followers of Jesus? For Christians, his resurrection accounts for this change.

Closely related to this line of evidence is the observation that in Jewish beliefs there was no requirement or expectation for Israel's Messiah to die and be raised from the dead. The death of Jesus did not suggest resurrection, as though resurrection following execution was part of a messianic paradigm. The death of a messianic contender invalidated the contender's claims.

As noted in chapter 5, we have at least ten examples of messianic and prophetic contenders (or pretenders) in the approximate time of Jesus. They promised one sign or another, assured their followers of deliverance and victory, and so forth. They were all defeated, and most of them were executed. Not one of their respective movements continued after their defeat and death. Yet the movement of Jesus did continue after his death. Why this exception? Christians believe the resurrection of Jesus can account for it.

Another line of argument goes to motivation. Again, what motivation could there have been to invent a story of resurrection? If Jesus died—especially at the hands of the Romans—then hopes pinned on him would have been viewed as clearly misplaced. Jesus' followers would simply continue in their Jewish faith, a faith focused on Israel's ancient stories of election and covenant, on Israel's famous temple and sacrificial system in Jerusalem, and on Israel's futuristic hope of eventual vindication and resurrection.

If Jesus had died and remained dead, there would have been no motivation to "revive" him. To cherish, preserve, and propagate his teaching would not require a resurrection any more than it did for all the great Jewish teachers. Here we can think of the great Rabbi Aqiba, who in the second century AD suffered martyrdom. His teaching lived on and was cherished, yet no one invented a story of his resurrection.

Historical Questions

A second line of evidence that supports the resurrection concerns historical questions. As I mentioned in chapter 1, no other religion comes close to Christianity with respect to the extent that one can test it against history.

In the world of Jesus and the early church—that is, the first, second, and third centuries AD—belief in resurrection from the dead was mocked and attacked by thinkers such as Celsus and Porphyry throughout the Roman Empire. If the disciples desired to create a new religion, they could not have chosen a more confusing place to start than inventing a narrative of a corpse coming to life. The early Christian movement should have died, along with its would-be founder.

But it did not. Why? The followers of Jesus claimed their founder was very much alive. There's little doubt that the main appeal of the Christian faith, the reason the church grew exponentially in the first few centuries, was its confidence in the face of death and the hope of a future bodily resurrection like that of its founder.

Christianity emerged in a world of immense suffering and low life expectancy. Life expectancy in the time of Jesus and the early church averaged only twenty years. Skeletal remains and other evidence suggest that on any given day as many as one-quarter of the Roman Empire population was sick, dying, or in need of immediate medical attention.

In general, only one-third of the skeletons found in archaeological digs from that time are those of adults. Infant mortality was as high as 30 percent; less than 49 percent of children saw their fifth birthday. Even in the glorious city of Rome, infant mortality was common. Near the catacomb of San Panfilo in Rome, 83 of the 111 graves are for children. Only 40 percent of the population lived to the age of twenty. It's not surprising, then, that Jesus, widely recognized as an extraordinary healer, attracted crowds (Mark 5:14; 6:56; 8:22; 10:13).

The resurrection narratives are found in all four Gospels and the book of Acts (Matthew 27:62–28:20; Mark 16:1–20; Luke 24:1–53; John 20–21; Acts 1:1–12). The Gospels are excellent sources, but they're not the earliest sources for the resurrection of Jesus. The apostle Paul is the best and earliest source for understanding when Christians came to believe in the bodily resurrection of Jesus. Paul also provides the details of the hope of the believer's own resurrection body. Although it's sometimes discounted, significant, credible eyewitness testimony does exist.

This testimony comes from those who believed in Jesus, from those who were indifferent toward him, and from at least two people who opposed him—James, his skeptical brother, and Saul of Tarsus, who even used violence. Moreover, these eyewitnesses were transformed by their encounter with the risen Jesus, none more dramatically than Saul, who became known as Paul the apostle.

Next let's turn to the written and archaeological sources that overwhelmingly support the Gospels' resurrection narrative.

8

Reason #5

*Written and Archaeological Sources
Overwhelmingly Support the Gospels'
Resurrection Narrative*

What do explorers, spies, espionage, MI6, the CIA, battles, attacks, in some cases death, bribery, thievery, defamation, lawsuits, and identity theft all have in common? Biblical archaeology! Archaeology is an adventure. It can also be dangerous, but oh so rewarding. (As for the danger, I know a Bible scholar who was denied an insurance policy when the company learned he was involved in archaeology.) Biblical archaeology is imperative for the study of the Old Testament, the New Testament, the historical Jesus, Jesus in Judaica, and Christian origins. There's no chance of understanding Jesus—or Paul or Peter—without understanding their New Testament world.

Archaeology as we know it today is a young discipline—only about 120 years old. The more modern techniques, such as wet sifting and dry sifting, and new sophisticated approaches are less than a hundred years old. Archaeology is history's closest cousin, and Christianity, unlike any other religion in the world, enjoys persuasive corroboration in the material culture. It can be shown that all other religious systems outside of Judaism and Christianity avoid any significant points of tangency with archaeology.

The Empty Tomb and Resurrection Appearance Tradition

The Greek text of the New Testament enjoys the support of significant evidence. The manuscript evidence is itself weighty. The manuscripts are early, numerous, and stable. Some small fragments date to the second century, while substantial portions of the text are preserved in manuscripts that date to the third century. The Gospel narratives themselves exhibit linguistic, archaeological, and cultural authenticity from the world of Jesus. They overlap with and are corroborated by several important sources.

As historians and biblical scholars, when we say the New Testament reflects the reality of the first-century world, we're noting that the contents of the biblical narrative correspond with what we know of the time and place these documents describe. In other words, the Bible finds its place in the ongoing cut and thrust of history, and there's tremendous overlap when one compares the sacred Judeo-Christian manuscripts with other surviving documents, inscriptions, and archaeological finds from antiquity. The four New Testament Gospels reflect early tradition and everywhere exhibit authenticity, which is what we should expect if they're truly credible historical sources. Another word for this authenticity is *verisimilitude*. In Latin, *veritas* (the root is *verus*, "truth") means "genuine" or "true"; *similitude* means "similarity" or "likeness."

The Gospels and New Testament epistles proclaim the principal elements of Christian faith: (1) Jesus showed himself alive after death, an element attested by the resurrection appearance tradition (1 Corinthians 15:3–7; 1 Thessalonians 1:9–10), and (2) Jesus abandoned the grave, an element attested by the empty-tomb tradition, which is known to all four Gospel evangelists (Matthew 28:1–8; Mark 16:1–8; Luke 24:1–12, 22–24; John 20:1–13).

On the archaeology of resurrection, we can raise several more flags. First, the Gospels themselves, in which the resurrection account is embedded. That Jesus' trial, conviction, death by crucifixion, and burial as well as the discovery of the empty tomb are all embedded in the Gospels exhibits verisimilitude.

I say this not just because they seem to agree with the times, the culture, and the historical sources. Specific archaeological discoveries indicate again and again that the Gospels are talking about real people, real places, real events. Indeed, specific things the Gospels discuss and describe have come to light. And so that leads us right away to the conclusion that the sources in which the Gospel narratives are recorded are reliable. They're not fairy tales. The narratives embedded in the Gospels are related to real places, real times, real people, and real events attested in a variety of sources.

Archaeology specifically related to the resurrection all centers on the tomb where Jesus' body was placed. The evidence suggests he was in fact removed from the cross and placed in a tomb. Some theories have been explored, but theories trotted out in recent years—some going back many years—suggest Jesus was probably not buried.

Archaeologically speaking, that's a ridiculous idea. Not even the Jewish high priest would allow any crucified person to hang on a cross overnight in the land of Israel, right outside the gates of Jerusalem, on the eve of Passover. That would be unthinkable. Scholars and archaeologists know that. Therefore, Jesus would have been placed in a real tomb. But what tomb?

According to Jewish law it could not be an honorable tomb. Jesus had been executed as a criminal, and both he and the two men crucified next to him would have to be placed in a tomb reserved for criminals. Jewish sources talk about such tombs, in fact, specifically linking them to the Sanhedrin. If the Sanhedrin condemned somebody to death, it fell to them to see to their proper burial. Please notice the description "proper burial," not "honorable burial." There should be no fanfare, no public lament, no public mourning—only a simple burial in a tomb.

This was the Sanhedrin's responsibility, and it's clearly taught in the earliest writings of the rabbis:

> They did not bury [the executed criminal] in the burying-place of his fathers. But two burying-places were kept in readiness *by the Sanhedrin*, one for them that were beheaded or strangled, and one for them that were stoned or burnt.[1] (Emphasis added; "strangled" would include those hanged and those crucified.)

The place reserved for burial of criminals was sometimes referred to as a "wretched place":

> Neither a corpse nor the bones of a corpse may be transferred from a wretched place to an honored place, nor, needless to say, from an honored placed to a wretched place; but if to the family tomb, even from an honored place to a wretched place, it is permitted.[2]

Not only was the body of a criminal not to be buried in a place of honor, but no public mourning for executed criminals was permitted: "They used not to make [open] lamentation . . . for mourning has place in the heart alone."[3] None of this law would make any sense if executed criminals were not in fact buried. There would have been no need to set aside tombs for executed criminals. There would simply be no remains to transfer from a "wretched place" to an "honored place."

What do the Gospels tell us? The Jewish Council was responsible to oversee the proper burial of the executed, because the bodies of the executed were normally not surrendered to family and friends. The burial of the executed in "wretched places," that is, in tombs set aside for criminals, was part of the punishment. No public mourning and lamentation were permitted. The remains of the executed could not be transferred from these dishonorable tombs for one year. After one year, the remains could be taken by family members to the family tomb or to some other place of honor.

The terse, almost matter-of-fact burial narrative we find in Mark 15 exhibits realism at every point. The narrative agrees with what is known of the relevant literature and archaeological data, both Jewish and Roman, both Palestinian and elsewhere in the empire. That the body of Jesus was taken down from the cross and placed in a known tomb, under the direction of someone acting on behalf of the Jewish Council, should be accepted as historical.

Precisely what the Gospels describe, this was a member of the Sanhedrin named Joseph of Arimathea. In fact, the Gospel of John adds a second member named Nicodemus. These two Sanhedrin members have sympathy for Jesus. They have pity for him. And so they see to his burial themselves.

Where is Jesus buried? Paul mentions the important fact that Jesus was buried (1 Corinthians 15:4), and this is where Joseph of Arimathea comes in: He gives Jesus a slightly better burial than otherwise would be expected. Jesus' body is placed not in a dishonorable tomb (with the corpses and skeletal remains of previously executed criminals) but in a brand-new tomb. It must be a new tomb, because if it's not a place of dishonor where criminals are buried, it can't be a place of honor where honorable people have been buried. But a new tomb—freshly hewn—is neutral. And so Jesus' body can be placed there.

This entire burial procedure has been reviewed by Jewish archaeologists, not only Christian archaeologists. Archaeologist Jodi Magness (University of North Carolina, Chapel Hill), has concluded that the New Testament Gospels get it right and are "consistent with archaeological evidence and with Jewish law."[4]

Jesus was buried, and the archaeology of Jewish burial customs supports the entire juridical procedure in the Gospel narratives. Jesus was buried in a known tomb, and according to Jewish custom, some timid, fearful women (the men had run away; what a mark of shame) come to the tomb at their first opportunity. What is the first opportunity? First light Sunday morning. Jesus dies and is buried before nightfall on Friday, Saturday is Shabbat, and the Sabbath ends Saturday night.

No one goes to tombs and cemeteries at night.

Rather, at first light, Sunday morning, the women visit. Why? Because the Jewish custom is to mourn *graveside* for an entire week, and Jesus hasn't been dead an entire week. And so the women come first thing Sunday morning with spices, not sure if Jesus' body had, in fact, been anointed. John's Gospel says it was, but these women don't know that. Why do they spice the body? Why do they perfume it? Because the body stinks. And because people can go inside tombs. Not that they always do, but they can go inside a tomb and mourn privately—grieve, sing songs, recite scriptures, pray.

From archaeology, we can actually see where places inside tomb floors were cut out lower, deeper into the ground so people could stand upright, which is the Jewish custom and posture of prayer—not to kneel as is typical among Christians but to stand upright and lift hands toward heaven. To lift one's face toward heaven and pray. This is exactly what the Gospels tell us the women plan to do. Their task is to perfume the body, mask the smell of death and decay, and pray.

But first they have to get inside the tomb, of course, and from skeletal remains we know that most women in Jesus' time were barely five feet tall and weighed not much more than in the nineties. So because the stone covering the entrance weighs several hundred pounds, these women are wondering who will help them roll it away.

At this point we interrupt the Gospel narrative to point out as best as we can tell from the surviving evidence—mostly physical and some written—that anywhere from 80 to 90 percent of stone doors sealing the entrance to a tomb in the land of Israel were, in fact, square or rectangular. They were large, heavy blocks that functioned similarly to a cork sealing or plugging a bottle. The archaeological remains show us that nearly all the entrances were around a meter square, and the body would have to be carried through the square horizontally.

As a critical thinker, you need to know that only 10, at most 20, percent of these stones would have been round in Jesus' day. Moderns have the impression that all the stone entrances were round then, but these larger stones were reserved for only the wealthy Jewish families who could afford the larger entrances and family tombs. Why? It was a practical amenity. It was easy to bring a couple of your servants to roll the large stone aside; indeed, some had an embedded track so the stone functioned more like a wheel. The smaller, square tomb stones would have to be lifted up and then pulled out like a stopper out of a bottle. This would have been very difficult and taken some effort even for men.[5]

The Gospels tell us Jesus is laid in a rich man's tomb (Matthew 27:57–60), and the women find the stone rolled aside. This is alarming. This doesn't necessarily mean the tomb has been violated, but at a minimum, it's been entered. One of the women's fears might be that the ruling priests didn't support what Joseph of Arimathea had done. We could speculate, perhaps, that those priests insisted that the body of Jesus be taken to a criminal's tomb, under the jurisdiction of the Sanhedrin. In any case, the women are alarmed when they find the tomb empty.

Where is Jesus?

Then the women have an amazing experience. They initially encounter someone they think is a gardener. At first glance, he's a young man, but then they realize he's an angel announcing that Jesus isn't there. In fact, he tells them they're not going to find his body anywhere in a tomb or cemetery and that Jesus has in fact been raised up (Matthew 28:5–7).

Established Facts

Here's the key to defending the resurrection of Jesus: We're free to say Jesus wasn't resurrected, but we're not free to disagree with established facts.

We're free to disagree with the women's experience and interpretation of the resurrection, saying, "Oh, perhaps they were mistaken or confused." But please understand that no one can support that decision based on the archaeology, or history, or the evidential record. They're simply disagreeing with the earliest reports and the earliest eyewitnesses. They're disagreeing with the very first witnesses—the actual people who experienced the resurrected Jesus—with the archaeological evidence, with history.

No, we're not free to disagree with the actual sources. We're not at liberty, intellectually, to make up some kind of story and say falsely, against all the evidence, that Jesus was not buried or that his body was thrown into a ditch and eaten by dogs (yet another theory). At that point, we're just making up our own sources and creating our own "facts" unhinged from the best evidence.

The facts are established: Jesus died on the cross, he was placed in a known tomb, and he was visited by women who were related to his followers and disciples. Much to their consternation, these women discovered that the tomb was open and Jesus' body was gone. And then they encountered an angelic visitor who knew why that was so and explained that Jesus was not there and had risen. The implication was, of course, that Jesus wasn't in any of the other tombs either. His body was nowhere to be found because he had been raised.

An interesting point, of course, is that some people in the first century didn't believe the women *because they were women.* But the male disciples saw Jesus as well.

Plenty of people didn't believe any of them and wanted to explain Jesus' body's disappearance in other ways. (Plenty of people still do.) Yet the body of Jesus never turned up. And if you understand Judaism, you know the bodies of the deceased, the bodies of loved ones, were precious. Keeping track of earthly remains was a sacred duty, making sure the bones eventually wound up, as they would be allowed to one year later (even the bones of criminals), in family tombs.

This is why over 150,000 bodies are buried on the Mount of Olives. There's no chance that Jesus' bones would just be disregarded and no one would worry about it, especially on the basis of a rumor that maybe Jesus was risen. After all, according to Jewish tradition, spirits could be raised up and appear to people. The Jewish people had their fair share of ghost stories. You didn't have to force the issue of resurrection to believe in a postmortem survival.

Why did Jesus' followers talk about resurrection and not simply the spirit of Jesus, who exists and lives today and reveals himself to us and makes us feel warm and loved? For two reasons.

First, because there was compelling evidence, against all expectation, that Jesus actually was raised up. That evidence is this: the empty tomb, no body found anywhere else, and no record that his body had been taken anywhere else.

Second, the resurrection appearances weren't mere ghost stories. Jesus wasn't a phantom you could look through. You could actually touch him. He could sit down at a table and eat. This was not a ghost. This was not a phantasmal experience. The only way his appearances could be explained was resurrection, and archaeology and other sources support this conclusion.

Post-Resurrection Appearances of Jesus

- To the women leaving the tomb area (Matthew 28:9-10)
- To Mary Magdalene (Mark 16:9-10; John 20:14-17)
- To two disciples on the road to Emmaus (Mark 16:12-13; Luke 24:13-31)
- To Peter (Luke 24:34; 1 Corinthians 15:5)
- To ten disciples in the upper room (Luke 24:36-49; John 20:19-23)
- To eleven disciples in the upper room (Mark 16:14; John 20:26-31; 1 Corinthians 15:5)
- To seven disciples fishing (John 21:1-23)
- To the disciples on a Galilee mountain (Matthew 28:16-20; Mark 16:15-18)
- To more than five hundred (1 Corinthians 15:6)
- To James and then all the apostles (1 Corinthians 15:7)
- At the ascension (Mark 16:19; Luke 24:50-51; Acts 1:7-9)
- To Paul (Acts 9:3-6)

9

Reason #6

Only Jesus' Resurrection Convincingly Explains the Conversion of People Not Previously His Followers

After his resurrection, Jesus appeared to those who believed in him, to those who doubted him, and to those who were opposed to him. What can't be contested is the fact that many of his earliest followers (two of them originally skeptics—Saul of Tarsus and Jesus' brother James) had resurrection experiences.

Indeed, they saw Jesus after his death, and due to this experience, they were willing to die proclaiming that very message. Jesus' disciples were willing to die because of a personal experience of encountering the resurrected Jesus, not what they'd heard or learned secondarily.

This resurrection experience emboldened them to carry the gospel (or "good news") throughout the Roman Empire with the conviction that God acted decisively through the Messiah,

Jesus Christ, through his incarnation, death, and resurrection from the dead, which Christians believe is sufficient to bring salvation to everyone.

As we continue to learn in this book, the Gospels and the book of Acts are excellent sources, but they're not the earliest source material for Jesus' resurrection. It's remarkable that the most important resurrection testimony comes from a previously hostile skeptic who did not follow Jesus during his ministry—Paul, formerly Saul of Tarsus. His account is found in 1 Corinthians 15:3–7:

> I delivered to you as of first importance what I also received: that Christ died for our sins in accordance with the Scriptures, that he was buried, that he was raised on the third day in accordance with the Scriptures, and that he appeared to Cephas, then to the twelve. Then he appeared to more than five hundred brothers at one time, most of whom are still alive, though some have fallen asleep. Then he appeared to James, then to all the apostles.

The source material for this creed is the oldest in the New Testament. It stretches back to within weeks of the resurrection event itself. The scholar James Dunn is "entirely confident" in stating that the tradition behind the composition of 1 Corinthians 15:3–4 was "formulated . . . within months of Jesus' death."[1] And professor Gary Habermas has compiled a comprehensive citation of biblical scholars from across the theological spectrum who agree on the early development of this central tradition.[2]

The apostle Paul declares that the resurrection of Jesus was a matter of "first importance" for Christian faith (1 Corinthians 15:3). In 1 Corinthians 15, he passed on the most important and earliest Christian tradition or creed to the Corinthian church in AD 53–55. This is the earliest declaration of faith in oral circulation before it was ever committed to writing.

We moderns also have creed-like statements. American students recite the Pledge of Allegiance: *I pledge allegiance to the flag of the United States of America and to the Republic for which it stands, one nation under God, indivisible, with liberty and justice for all.* And "The Star-Spangled Banner" begins most major sporting events in the United States. A creed is defined as a formal statement of Christian beliefs. In the Old Testament, the Shema prayer (Deuteronomy 6:4–9, "Hear, O Israel . . .") could be characterized as a creedal statement and has for centuries functioned as such for the Jewish people.

Paul didn't invent the creed found in 1 Corinthians 15. That's evident when he says, "I handed on to you . . . what I in turn had received" (verse 3 NRSV). Earlier in his letter (chapter 11, verse 23), Paul used the same formulaic language—"I received from the Lord what I also delivered to you"—in describing how the church should conduct the Lord's Supper. Paul was passing on traditions that predated not only his letter to the Corinthian church—containing what early Christians came to believe about the resurrection and also when they believed it—but that predated his own conversion.

Paul wrote thirteen of the twenty-seven New Testament books, constituting nearly 25 percent of the New Testament. Of all that he wrote, none is of greater importance for Christian faith than what he passes on in 1 Corinthians 15. In verse 3, Paul makes clear what is at stake by asserting that the bodily resurrection of Jesus is a matter "of first importance." The resurrection of Jesus was the pivotal point of the new faith.

Understanding this early passage is the key to understanding the theology of Paul and the entire New Testament. It also answers the skeptic who claims that the resurrection story of Jesus is a fable created in the years and decades after his death. The Greco-Roman culture of the first century did not understand how or why anyone could or would believe that a corpse could live again. The proclamation of the early Christian leaders that the dead Jesus did in fact come back to life would have been strange and off-putting to any Greek or Roman.

This is most likely why Paul was mocked on Mars Hill for proclaiming the resurrection (Acts 17:32). This negative reaction is also seen among Christians in Corinth, perhaps influenced by the Platonic notion of the soul, who persisted in their belief that there was no resurrection. It is for this reason that Paul found it necessary to pen 1 Corinthians 15.

Paul—the Earliest Source for the Resurrection

After his conversion, Saul of Tarsus became Paul the apostle. But as Saul, he was known for persecuting Christians individually and attacking the early Christian movement, or "the Way" (Acts 7). Unlike the other apostles, Paul met Jesus after the resurrection. The rest experienced Jesus prior to his passion and resurrection, but Paul knew Jesus *as* the resurrection.

How did Paul come to this unshakable, unquenchable belief in Jesus and the resurrection? He passed on an early Christian creed (1 Corinthians 15:3–5) to the Corinthian church in AD 53–55. It's known in biblical scholarship as the *kerygma*: "the message, or proclamation or preaching."[3] The earliest kerygma was in circulation orally before it was ever committed to writing. These early creeds preserved the Christian faith before the New Testament was written.

It's important to remember that early Christians did not have a "Bible" as we know Scripture today. For this reason, these early creeds and hymns were extremely important for emerging Christianity. When did Paul receive this kerygma (proclamation), this creed, this resurrection material he passed on to the church of Corinth? Nero's persecution of him is a helpful datum.

The infamous and psychotic emperor Nero, who reigned from AD 54 to AD 68, martyred the apostle Paul around AD 65 (Peter was also most likely martyred by Nero in AD 65). Nero's persecution of Christians began in AD 64. This is an important point, because obviously Paul wrote all his epistles prior to his martyrdom.

Paul was converted to Christianity about one or two years after the crucifixion and resurrection of Jesus.[4] As I said in chapter 1, we can pinpoint the date of the crucifixion and resurrection on Friday, April 7–9, AD 30 (some think April 3–5, AD 33). According to Galatians 1:18–19, Paul visited Jerusalem three years after his conversion on the road to Damascus.

What was Paul doing for those three years? In verse 17 of Galatians 1, he says he went first to Arabia to spend time with God, probably in prayer, study, and meditation. He decided to go to God first rather than "consult any human being" (verse 16 NIV), even the other apostles. Then after three years, he traveled to Jerusalem sometime in the mid AD 30s to "visit Cephas and remained with him fifteen days" (verse 18 NIV).

The Greek word for "visit" is *historeo*, which is similar to our English word *history*. It's used outside the Bible to describe people who investigate. Our English translation "to become acquainted" (NASB) or "to visit" (ESV) with Peter doesn't do justice to the force of the Greek. Paul was carefully studying and critically thinking about Jesus' resurrection with two of the most important early eyewitnesses: Peter and James (Jesus' brother), both of whom he met in Jerusalem. Historically speaking, Paul was in the right place at the right time. This is where he received the kerygma.

Paul wasn't the only skeptic to claim to have an experience of a personal appearance of the risen Jesus. His brother James did.

The Gospels report that no one in Jesus' family (with the exception of his mother, Mary) "believed" he was the long-awaited Messiah. Family and friends in his hometown, Nazareth, asked, "Is not this the carpenter, the son of Mary and brother of James and Joses and Judas and Simon? And are not his sisters here with us?" And then the Bible says, "They took offense at him" (Mark 6:3).

Then a few chapters earlier we learn that Jesus' family is embarrassed by him: "When his family heard it, they went out to seize him, for they were saying, 'He is out of his mind'" (Mark 3:21). And elsewhere we're told that "not even his brothers believed in him" (John 7:5).

Prior to the appearance of the risen Jesus to him (1 Corinthians 15:7), James was not a follower of his brother. Following his experience with the risen Jesus, however, James was willing to die for the brother he now regarded as the resurrected Messiah. Josephus provides a detailed and lengthy history of the Jewish people. He records that James, "the brother of Jesus called the Messiah," was stoned to death illegally by the Sanhedrin in AD 62.[5] In view of this evidence, the careful student must ask this contextual question: What would it take for one to die a violent death for believing one's brother was the resurrected Messiah?

Therefore, the power that united the apostles, launched the first church, and finally overwhelmed the Roman Empire was the deeply held conviction that Jesus had physically risen from the dead. As the evangelist Luke puts in his history of the first century of the church, "With great power the apostles continued to testify to the resurrection of the Lord Jesus. And God's grace was so powerfully at work in them all" (Acts 4:33 NIV). In Romans 1:4, Paul proclaimed that Jesus "was declared the Son of God with power . . . by the resurrection from the dead" (NASB).

Without the resurrection, there would be no good news for the apostles of Jesus to preach. Without it, the New Testament's content, narrative, and teaching would make little sense.

The Jewish Context of Paul's Conversion

Saul of Tarsus (later known as Paul) was a pious Jew who believed in the general eschatological resurrection. He was a

Pharisee. He believed in Israel's legacy. He believed the people of God were in fact chosen. He believed in a future vindication someday. And Saul of Tarsus was outraged over Christianity.

To be clear, he wasn't outraged because these Jews who were now Jesus followers believed the man was resurrected so much as he was outraged because they were teaching about the resurrection and Jesus in an open form of evangelization. They now believed in an open community where gentiles were welcome. And it was not required that gentiles convert in the usual pharisaic understanding. They didn't have to eat kosher food. They didn't have to get circumcised. And Saul saw this as a threat.

Indeed, he interpreted this as an existential threat to the future of Israel. This surely would corrupt Israel. At some point this would probably result in God's judgment upon the nation. They had fought the Greeks in the second century BC, the Maccabean uprising against the Seleucids in the north who wanted them to conform and be more gentile-like and eat non-kosher food. Therefore, the martyrs of the second century BC fought against these heresies and paid with their lives.

Saul is appalled by what he sees in Christianity. He sees Christianity, therefore, as a threat, a corruption, a heresy: *Jesus surely wasn't raised up. He was no messiah. How could he be? When the true Messiah comes, the gentiles will die.*

Saul's Conversion Shook the Roman Empire

When Saul of Tarsus is on the road to Damascus, he's convinced Jesus wasn't raised up. Jesus' teaching and theology is faulty. It results in including non-Torah-observant gentiles in the Jewish community. Obviously, that's a blasphemy. Obviously, that will lead to bad things. It will corrupt the community. It will nullify the covenant of Sinai. It will make righteousness in the Jewish context impossible. Or so went the thinking of Saul, who in the Bible is called Paul after his conversion. (As a reminder, it was customary for Jews who were Roman citizens to use two names reflecting the Aramaic and Latin languages, which in this case are Saul and Paul.)

Then he dramatically meets the risen Jesus on the road, and that changes everything. But he doesn't just say, *Oh, now I believe Jesus is resurrected. Now I believe he's the Messiah.* This conversion means an embracing of Jesus' whole agenda. That he goes from a narrow-minded chauvinistic misanthropist to a man called Paul who loves all of humanity. The vision of Jesus so changes him that he writes these words in Galatians 3:28: "With Christ . . . there is neither Jew nor Greek" (NIV).

Do you realize how revolutionary that is? No Pharisee could ever say those words. In Messiah Jesus, in Christ Jesus, there's neither Jew nor Greek. And in the same verse Paul says, "neither slave nor free." Those sentiments will surely shake the economics and society of Rome to its foundation.[6] In Christ, Paul also says in that verse, there is in fact "neither male nor female." All three of those statements would be considered outrageous in both Jewish and gentile circles.

Where did this innovative view of equality, this lightning bolt, come from? No teachers—Greek or Jewish—and no philosophers or rabbis were teaching such crazy stuff. It came from Paul's encounter with the risen Christ. Please don't miss the point: Paul doesn't just come to believe *Oh, Jesus is the Son of God after all, the Messiah after all, and his resurrection was necessary after all. In fact, his resurrection really happened.* No. It's more.

This experience converts Paul from the top of his head to the ends of his toes. He buys into the entire Jesus program. A program that lionizes women. That implies egalitarian principles. That loves children. Every child in Jesus' economy is in fact a wanted child. All people are wanted. There's no racism. The Syrophoenician woman is a gentile (Mark 7:24–30), yet she can be blessed too. Samaritans can be blessed and so forth.

Paul buys into the whole Jesus program because of the resurrection. He's transformed. Theologically speaking, he didn't need a resurrection to be a Jew and a Pharisee. But when he encountered the resurrected Jesus, again, it changed everything.

For me and hopefully for you, this is significant and weighty evidence. Paul was hostile to Christianity. Then Paul, who from his point of view did not believe in or need the resurrection, encountered the risen Christ and was transformed—totally.

And what is the result for us? Paul's letters are the most influential ever written. Under the agency and leadership of the Holy Spirit, they transformed the whole world, especially in the West, where the Christian message was heard and embraced.

Paul's letters transformed barbarian Europe into a civilization and society more advanced than the East. The early Christian movement influenced most of the Roman Empire in a rather short of period of time. Belief in the bodily resurrection of Jesus was the driving force behind the growth and expansion of the early church from 120 people in the upper room to a movement that, by the time it had reached Greece in Thessalonica, had "turned the world upside down" (Acts 17:6).

There's More

Luke, Paul's traveling companion and the author of Acts, is also a key source about the resurrection. Every sermon recorded in Acts discusses the resurrection of Jesus. (Twenty-two percent of that book is dialogue.)

And in my book *Unanswered*, I wrote this on the Resurrection-centrism in Paul's writings:

> In the opening verses of Romans, Paul gloriously states that Jesus "was declared to be the Son of God in power . . . by the resurrection from the dead" (1:4). To the Philippians, Paul said,

"I want to know Christ and experience the mighty power that raised him from the dead" (3:10 NLT).

More than two dozen times in the New Testament, followers of Jesus are promised they will be raised with Jesus. No other promise occurs with more frequency than the assurances of the believer's resurrection because it's linked with Jesus' personal resurrection (Romans 6:4; 8:11; compare Ephesians 2:6).

The early Christian message had a potency and relevance; it was not exclusive but inclusive and accepting of all classes, no matter one's social demographic. The early church was resurrection-centric in all its teaching and mission.[7]

10

Reason #7

Jesus' Resurrection Is the Only Basis for Making Sense of Suffering

Steve Jobs was one of the most iconic people of our time. His innovations have shaped and connected the world. No wonder he appeared on the cover of *Time* eight times between 1982 and 2011.

At thirteen years of age, Jobs had an unanswered question that tragically caused him to walk away from his Christian faith. Author and journalist Walter Isaacson wrote these chilling words about the young man's experience:

> In July 1968 *Life* magazine published a shocking cover showing a pair of starving children in Biafra. Jobs took it to Sunday school and confronted the church's pastor. "If I raise my finger, will God know which one I'm going to raise even before I do it?" The pastor answered, "Yes, God knows everything." Jobs then pulled out the *Life* cover and asked, "Well, does God know about this and what's going to happen to those children?"

"Steve, I know you don't understand, but yes, God knows about that." Jobs announced that he didn't want to have anything to do with worshipping such a God, and he never went back to church.[1]

What questions have you had about the existence of evil and suffering in the world? Perhaps the most prevalent unanswered question people have today is the question of tragedy, pain, and suffering. As Christian thinkers, we must be prepared to answer these questions for the young Steve Jobses of the world.

Have your questions about evil and suffering ever led you to question your faith in God, as Jobs did? If so, how did that affect your faith journey? Without the resurrection of Jesus, we have no answer for the suffering in the world.

Suffering is the wake-up call you didn't ask for and the nightmare that quickly becomes reality. Suffering, in rapid speed, can take you back to being five years old and experiencing the utter terror of riding a bike without training wheels for the first time. Are you going to pedal, steer, and maneuver through this challenge in life without taking a massive tumble?

Suffering is like a mirror that reveals who we really are. Sometimes it's hard to recognize ourselves in the midst of trials. Suffering is mysterious, often surfacing at the wrong times, in the wrong places, and with the wrong people. Suffering is a noun and a verb and a full stop all together. Suffering is both self-explanatory and unexplainable. Suffering is a problem we all face at one time or another. Suffering can't be unfriended; it's personal, local, regional, and long distance. Suffering is the most common human experience, and it changes most of us forever.

Suffering is an eternal unanswered question the Bible has an answer for and, with the correct theology, can be viewed as an incredible opportunity. So what is it about suffering that stops us in our tracks and almost paralyzes us with panic? Is it that we're weak, needy, and terrified of pain? Or do we wonder deep down inside whether God will truly make good on his promise to be there for us (Hebrews 13:5)?

C. S. Lewis revealed pertinent insight when asked about pain and suffering: "We are not necessarily doubting that God will do the best for us; we are wondering how painful the best will turn out to be."[2]

How do we answer the unanswered questions of suffering in our own mind as well as in the minds of our family, friends, and coworkers? Did you know that because of the resurrection, we can (and should) discuss our loved ones who have died in the Lord in the present tense? This is the great promise of the resurrection of Jesus: "Because I live, you also will live" (John 14:19).

Are you strong? Are you immovable? Are you excelling in good works?

Perhaps you, like Peter, have failed. The resurrection shows us God loves second chances.

Perhaps you're like Mary and Martha in John 11—you've lost someone, and the grief literally takes your breath away. You say with these two sisters, "Lord, if only you had been here" (verse 21 NIV). Perhaps you're like James—Jesus' brother—a skeptic unconvinced. Perhaps you're like Saul of Tarsus—outright hostile to the Christian faith. The resurrection strikes at the heart of every person because we all live in a world of suffering.

We live in a society that has given in to despair, that's lost hope. Scores of people wonder, *What is the point of life?* But the resurrection is what gives us hope. According to Jesus, it gives us purpose. Your whole life can be poured out in a God-serving way. That's what the resurrection does for us. We are and continue to become the people who bring hope. This first line of evidence from Paul in Romans 8:18 helps us learn why we can have hope in the face of the most difficult odds: "I consider that the sufferings of this present time are not worth comparing with the glory that is to be revealed to us."

If you knew with certainty that you would live forever, what would you do differently? What risks would you take?

Paul's Letters Affirm Christian Faith Based on Jesus' Resurrection

If the resurrection never happened, the apostle Paul said, then the early Christians might as well have stopped suffering for Christ (compare Romans 12:1–2) and dedicated their lives to pleasure (1 Corinthians 15:30–32). But since Jesus *has* been raised, Paul stated, Christians should pursue holy living (compare 15:33–34). Though Paul didn't endorse baptism for the dead, he pointed out that the practice (evidently existent in Corinth, according to works predating the Pauline epistles) is meaningless if there is no resurrection (1 Corinthians 15:29).[3]

From the beginning, Christianity appears to teach that resurrection isn't something to be embarrassed about but to proclaim and, if need be, sacrifice one's life for. If the late Second Temple period produced a new literary genre known as *martyrology*, Christianity gave it a new meaning by devising its own term—*martys* (literally "witness," or transliterated "martyr").[4] The New Testament portrays God's vindication of the first martyr, the Lord, by raising him from the dead. Jesus is called the firstfruits of the general resurrection through this vindication and promises eternal vindication for his followers at the final resurrection.

Paul's Letters Describe Early Christians' Actions Based on Jesus' Resurrection

As mentioned earlier, Paul was converted to Christianity in the early AD 30s or "about two years after the crucifixion of Jesus."[5]

And again, according to Galatians 1:18–19, Paul visited Jerusalem three years after his conversion on the road to Damascus: "After three years I went up to Jerusalem to visit Cephas and remained with him fifteen days. But I saw none of the other apostles except James the Lord's brother." It's plausible that Paul received this early tradition from the Lord's brother and Cephas within five years of said event.

The Pauline letters also describe the nature of the Christian understanding of bodily resurrection. The resurrection is an organic body (1 Corinthians 15:35: "body"). Paul responds to the foolish person's question, "How are the dead raised?" (1 Corinthians 15:35), with a multi-layered response. The hypothetical questioner is answered by an agricultural example (verses 36–38), a delineation of the similarities and differences of earthly and heavenly, or resurrected, bodies (verses 39–44), and finally with a clarion call of hope pointed at the resurrected last Adam (verse 49): "We shall also bear the image of the man of heaven." From this tradition, we can determine that early Christians believed the resurrected body would be more glorious than the present one.

In addition, the Pauline resurrection foretells cosmic signs and miracles hastening the resurrection of the dead. In 1 Corinthians 15:52 we're told the dead will rise in a moment ("in a flash" in the NIV), in a "twinkling of an eye," and loud noises accompany this apocalyptic hastening of the dead "at the last trumpet." And as I said in chapter 6, in his epistle to the Thessalonians, Paul states these are the different sounds that will be heard at the resurrection: the "cry of command" of "the Lord himself," "the voice of an archangel," and "the trumpet of God" (1 Thessalonians 4:16).

I wrote this in my book *Unanswered*, explaining more about how resurrection belief informed the early Christians' actions:

Within a Greco-Roman culture that viewed resurrection belief as disgusting, the early Christian movement thrived in their resurrection-centric faith. Resurrection belief drove the Christians to value all life, which included caring for the body in burial. It's unsurprising that Christians desired to be buried together; however, they innovated a new term related to their burial practices—*cemetery*—because death was peacefully thought of as rest or sleep, a temporary holding place.[6]

The stratigraphy [geological evidence] of the distinctively Christian "cemetery" was similar to the common *necropolis*, with an added eschatological dimension associated with bodily resurrection. This is noteworthy in that early Christian burial terminology had an inherent eschatological perspective in contrast to the wider Roman terminology for burial (compare a *mausoleum* for the wealthy or a *sepulcrum* for placing one's ashes). Perhaps the closest Latin comparison to the early Christian cemetery would be *monumentum*, which is most likely related to *moneo*, *monere* "to advise or remind," in special recognition of a life.

Body dumping was a significant problem in Rome, and it's been estimated that at least fifteen hundred corpses were abandoned.[7] Corpses of the destitute, slave, and poor were thrown in mass pits or *petuculi* forgotten to eternity.[8] The fact that early Christians cared for each individual body in burial, because of a resurrection-centric faith, could account for the rapid spread of the movement among the poor and slave classes in the Roman Empire.[9]

What Does the Bible Say about a Christian's Death?

The Bible says so many wonderful things about the death of a Christian. Psalm 116:15 states, "Precious in the sight of the LORD is the death of his saints." One of the most comforting statements regarding the death of any Christian who has trusted the Lord is this: "A Christian life isn't perfect, just forgiven."

Once a person comes to know Jesus Christ through an act of faith, receiving the forgiveness of sin he so bountifully offers, there's not one sin a believer can commit that will keep him or her out of heaven. In Romans 8:35, 37–39 (KJV) we're told:

> Who shall separate us from the love of Christ? Shall tribulation, or distress, or persecution, or famine, or nakedness, or peril, or sword? . . . Nay, in all these things we are more than conquerors through him that loved us. For I am persuaded, that neither death, nor life, nor angels, nor principalities, nor powers, nor things present, nor things to come, nor height, nor depth, nor any other creature, shall be able to separate us from the love of God, which is in Christ Jesus our Lord.

Have you had a specific moment, a specific time in your life, when you trusted in Christ as your savior?

On the authority of God's Word, we can say that right now our loved ones who died following Christ are in his presence in heaven. But how can we be so sure? Second Corinthians tells us that to be absent from the body is to be present with the Lord (5:8). And on the cross, Jesus looked at the thief dying next to him, the one who had expressed faith in him, and said, "Truly, I say to you, today you will be with me in paradise" (Luke 23:43).

A few days before his death, the great preacher Dr. F. B. Meyer wrote to a dear friend, "I have just heard, to my great surprise, that I have but a few days to live. It may be that before this reaches you, I shall have entered the palace. Don't trouble to write. We shall meet in the morning."[10] And Dr. William Carey, the great father of modern missions, wrote in his biography, "When I am gone, say nothing about Dr. Carey, speak about Dr. Carey's Savior."[11]

For the believer, death means entering into the glorious presence of Christ. But we must not think that all the past blessings with our loved ones are gone when their death comes. No, the memories linger, and more than that, the person who listens to the gospel, repents of sin, and turns to Christ in personal trust lives beyond physical death. Indeed, many of us have had to muster up those words "Good-bye for now." But under much better circumstances, we can say "Good morning"—when we're called to see Jesus and our loved ones face-to-face.

How can this be? Who gives victory over death? Who makes it possible for our sins to be forgiven? Who takes away the power of evil and grants life everlasting? The answer is this: God's Son and our Savior, the Lord Jesus Christ. In John 11:25–26, he said, "I am the resurrection and the life. Whoever believes in me, though he die, yet shall he live, and everyone who lives and believes in me shall never die. Do you believe this?"

The background to this statement was the death of Lazarus, a dear friend of Jesus Christ. I mentioned this story in chapter 6. Lazarus and his two sisters, Martha and Mary, lived in the small village of Bethany, which is about two miles from Jerusalem and situated on the eastern slopes of the Mount of Olives. Bethany was a serene country setting. The villagers worked hard and long in the vegetable and grain fields of the valleys in that vicinity.

Lazarus and his sisters were all devout believers in the Lord. They studied and obeyed the directives of the Word of God. They saw in Jesus the promised Messiah, whose life and ministry had been so clearly prophesied in the Jewish scriptures. When Jesus came to Jerusalem, they offered him a place to live and food at their house. But on the occasion of the narrative of our text, this lovely scene had turned into a tragic one with great grief.

Lazarus, Jesus' beloved friend, had suddenly taken ill and died. Although messengers had sent for Jesus, it was four days after the death and burial of Lazarus before he arrived. The sisters knew Jesus had the power to heal the sick, and they had hoped he would make it to their house in time to heal their brother.

But it was too late. Lazarus was dead. He'd been buried for four days. For the time being, it was a hopeless scene. And in the midst of their grief, both Martha and Mary had forgotten that Jesus not only healed the sick but raised the dead. (This reminds me that in moments of grief, we need to stake our lives on faith, not on feelings.) So when Jesus arrived, though he met Martha and Mary at separate times, Mary the last, they each said to him, "Lord, if you had been here, my brother would not have died" (John 11:21, 32).

Verses 33 and 34 tell us, "When Jesus saw [Mary] weeping, and the Jews who had come with her also weeping, he was deeply moved in his spirit and greatly troubled. And he said, 'Where have you laid him?'" This is the juncture where we read one of the shortest verses in all the Bible, verse 35: "Jesus wept."

Yet earlier, in response to the sisters' sorrowful statements, Jesus was already turning their hopelessness back to hopefulness: "I am the resurrection and the life. He who believes in Me, though he may die, he shall live. And whoever lives and believes in Me shall never die. Do you believe this?" (John 11:25–26 NKJV).

That same Scripture passage reassures *us* that Jesus continues to be

The Person of Hope
The Power of Hope
The Prerequisite of Hope
The Promise of Hope
The Permanence of Hope

The Person of Hope: "I Am"

This "I Am" statement is not simply a noun with a verb of being; it's the title of the eternal and self-existent God. But he has no name, per se. Yes, because the Hebrew word for "he is" or "he exists" is *yahweh* (the word that appears in Exodus 3), the God of the Bible is regularly identified as Yahweh, as though a proper name. In the Greek, this name is regularly translated as *kyrios*, which means "Lord." In fact, because Yahweh is so sacred that devout Jews are reluctant to speak it, the Hebrew word *adonai*, which also means "Lord," is often used in its place.

But the important thing to remember is that the God of the Bible, the God of the patriarchs Abraham, Isaac, and Jacob, has no name like the other gods of great antiquity. He is simply "I Am." The "One Who Is," the ground of all being, the Creator and Sustainer of all life. The uniqueness of God, the fact that there is no other god, means that God has no need for a "name" that distinguishes him from other the gods because no other gods exist.

The Power of Hope: "I Am the Resurrection"

The power that spoke the universe into existence is Jesus Christ. He is the power that caused the blind to see, the lame to walk, the deaf to hear, the mute to talk, the dead to live, the storms to calm. The power of Jesus Christ is dedicated to our deliverance, forgiveness, and salvation. Paul wrote to the Romans, "I am not ashamed of the gospel of Christ, for it is the power of God to salvation for everyone who believes, for the Jew first and also for the Greek" (Romans 1:16 NKJV). And in John 14:19 Jesus promised, "Because I live, you also will live."

This is our hope—Jesus Christ will freely forgive our sins and we will live with him in heaven for all eternity.

The Prerequisite of Hope: "Do You Believe This?"

Many things in life are unattainable, but we can all believe in Christ. These are key Scriptures that tell us so:

But as many as received Him, to them He gave the right to become children of God, to those who believe in His name.

John 1:12 NKJV

Believe on the Lord Jesus Christ, and you will be saved, you and your household.

Acts 16:31 NKJV

Most assuredly, I say to you, he who hears My word and believes in Him who sent Me has everlasting life, and shall not come into judgment, but has passed from death into life.

John 5:24 NKJV

If you confess with your mouth the Lord Jesus and believe in your heart that God has raised Him from the dead, you will be saved. For with the heart one believes unto righteousness, and with the mouth confession is made unto salvation.

Romans 10:9–10 NKJV

Faith isn't complicated. Again, have you placed your trust in Jesus Christ? Have you had a moment when you made a conscious, willful decision to turn to him?

The Promise of Hope: "He Shall Live"

The great promise of the resurrection is that in the same moment we take our last breath on earth, we are in face-to-face communion with our Lord: "To be absent from the body [is] to be present with the Lord" (2 Corinthians 5:8 NKJV). And Romans 6:23 says, "The free gift of God is eternal life in Jesus Christ our Lord." And the words that came off the lips of Jesus Christ himself ring true in our hearts: "Whoever believes in me, though he die, yet shall he [most certainly] live" (John 11:25).

Jesus set out again and again to show his power over death, sin, and Satan, whether through resurrection or resuscitation. In John 11:43, he called out to Lazarus, who had been dead for four days, "Lazarus, come out." And verse 44 tells us, "The man who had died came out."

The Permanence of Hope: "Shall Never Die"

Jesus didn't just stop with the miracle of raising Lazarus. He continued with this rock-sold promise in John 11:26 (NKJV): "And whoever lives and believes in Me shall never die. Do you believe this?" When we make a choice to place our trust in Jesus Christ, the eternal person of God comes to live inside our spirit, guaranteeing that we will live eternally with him. When death comes to our door, it can take only the body, not the soul. And because Jesus Christ is the resurrection, we have the guarantee that we will be resurrected with a new heavenly body someday—a body that will never grow tired, grow old, or see decay. We're even promised there will be no more tears (Revelation 21:4).

Once more, the important question for today is this: Have you received Jesus Christ? You're not a Christian because you go to church, or because you're a good person, or because you've kept the Golden Rule. Being a Christian is all about being forgiven, but you must invite God in. He's a gentleman; he will not force you. But in Jesus Christ we find forgiveness for sin, peace with God, and eternal resurrection life. The teaching that salvation is conditioned solely on faith appears over two hundred times in the New Testament. Works are a grace-killing element. The only thing you can bring to the cross has already been brought there: your sins. Have you placed your trust in Jesus Christ for your forgiveness of sin and eternal life with him? You can do that right now. Trust in Christ.

+ + +

As we have learned in this book, that Jesus Christ rose from the dead is an empirical claim. Christianity is utterly unique from other religions in that you can test the claims and beliefs because they are falsifiable and verifiable. We can trust in the resurrection of Jesus because of—not in spite of—the evidence. Non-Christian philosopher of religion Antony Flew (with whom Gary Habermas, author of the foreword for this book, debated) stated, "The evidence for the resurrection is better than for claimed miracles in any other religion. It's outstandingly different in quality and quantity."[12]

In part 4, I take you more deeply into scholarly resurrection research. But as I conclude this chapter, I hope my prayers and goals for this book have already been realized: reclaiming a Jesus resurrection-centric faith.

And again, I pray *Body of Proof* is a tool you can return to over and over, reminding you of the powerful evidence for the gospel. Also, I pray you've been encouraged to seek out the transformational difference living out a resurrection-centric life makes.

PART FOUR

The NEW FRONTIER: FURTHER ASSESSING *the* EVIDENCE

11

The Most Significant Place in Christianity

For all the Bible students who love Jesus' resurrection, I refer to these next two chapters as "the new frontier" in resurrection research. They're a more scholarly treatment of ways we can argue for the authenticity and historicity of Jesus' resurrection. My prayer is that they will equip you to move the conversation forward even more.

Every year, hundreds of thousands of Christians visit two tombs in Jerusalem believed to be where Jesus was buried after his crucifixion. The vast majority visit the Church of the Holy Sepulchre, an ancient church cared for by the Roman Catholics, Greek Orthodox, Armenian Apostolic Church, and in minor roles, the Coptic Orthodox, Syrian Orthodox, and Ethiopic Orthodox. The second place scholars consider was Christ's tomb is the Garden Tomb, which tends to be visited primarily by Protestants.

Which of these two tombs, if either, actually held Christ's body? The findings of archaeology help us answer this question.

The Garden Tomb (Gordon's Golgotha)

Of the two competing sites, the Garden Tomb—also called Gordon's Golgotha—is the most scenic. Those who see it can easily imagine what the tomb of Jesus would have looked like. But is it the tomb where Jesus was buried?

In 1841, British explorer Edward Robinson published *Biblical Researches in Palestine*, which provided a detailed account of his recent visit to the Holy Land.[1] He argued against the Church of the Holy Sepulchre as the authentic location of the tomb of Jesus because it was located within the walls of the Old City. According to Jewish custom, the dead were to be buried outside the city. Robinson suggested that the authentic tomb would be located near the Damascus road, two hundred meters or so from the Damascus Gate. Protestants welcomed his rejection of the traditional site and began searching for an alternate location.

Following the publication of Robinson's work, other early explorers identified a hill that resembled the face of a skull, complete with two eye sockets, a triangular shaped nose cavity, and a crevice that resembled the upper part of a mouth. This "Skull Hill" was identified as Calvary (in Latin) or Golgotha (in Aramaic; see Matthew 27:33; Mark 15:22; John 19:17). The new site was popular because of its proximity to the Antonia Fortress, where Jesus likely stood before Pilate. In 1874, Conrad Schick investigated a nearby tomb, which included a carved trench that served as a guide for a round stone. A nearby olive press apparently corresponded with the ancient name Gethsemane, Aramaic for "olive press" (compare Matthew 26:36; Mark 14:32).

Because some early church fathers believed that Jesus was buried near the place where he prayed, the presence of the olive press was seen as support for the identification of Skull Hill as Calvary and the tomb with the trench, or groove, as the tomb of Joseph of Arimathea, in which the body of Jesus was interred. Major-General Charles Gordon visited Jerusalem in 1883, and influenced by Schick, he warmly embraced the proposed new location. His allegorical appeals to certain passages of Scripture, as well as his curious "skeletal diagram" of Jerusalem in which the skeleton's skull happened to correspond with Skull Hill, convinced many that the Garden Tomb was indeed the actual tomb of Jesus.

Archaeological study, however, has not supported the Garden Tomb. The main problem is that it's much too old to be the "new" tomb Joseph of Arimathea made available (Matthew 27:60; compare Luke 23:53). According to Israeli archaeologist Gabriel Barkay, the Garden Tomb could date as early as the seventh or eighth century BC.[2] Some date it to the Hellenistic period (perhaps fourth century BC).

Either way, the Garden Tomb is much too old. Archaeologists point out that the architecture of the Garden Tomb doesn't match that of the tombs from the time of Jesus, for which we have many examples. Moreover, the carved trench, or groove, in front of the entrance to the Garden Tomb is medieval and was carved by Crusaders as a water trough for livestock, not a groove that guided a round stone. The olive press is a cistern, and it, too, was likely constructed by Crusaders, as indicated by the type of plaster.

Nor does geological research support the Garden Tomb as the place where Jesus was buried. The "skull" face of Skull Hill, very popular with today's tourists, has eroded a great deal in the century and a half since its identification. Comparison with old photographs makes that quite apparent. What the hill would have resembled two thousand years ago, if anything, is anyone's guess. It's most unlikely that it looked like it does now. Indeed, in a few decades there may well be nothing left of the eerie skull-like face.

For these reasons, few defenders of the Garden Tomb as the authentic site of Jesus' burial exist today. Even the Garden

Tomb Association that cares for the site admits that the tomb probably was not the tomb of Jesus.

But if archaeological and geological study does not support the Garden Tomb, does it support the tomb inside the Church of the Holy Sepulchre (pictured on the cover of this book)?

Church of the Holy Sepulchre

The archaeology of the Church of the Holy Sepulchre is fascinating. The Gospels agree that Jesus was buried in a tomb belonging to Joseph of Arimathea (Matthew 27:57; Luke 23:50–51; John 19:38) and that after Jesus' burial the entrance to the tomb was sealed with a stone. Luke 23:53 gives us the specific detail that the tomb was hewn from stone, and Matthew 27:60 and John 19:41 indicate it was a new tomb. Matthew adds that Joseph had meant the tomb for himself. John 19:41–42 states that the tomb was in a garden near the place where Jesus was crucified and that the place of execution was "near the city" (John 19:20). From the epistle to the Hebrews, it's clear that it was outside the walls of Jerusalem at the time: Jesus suffered "outside the gate" (Hebrews 13:12; here the author of Hebrews draws an analogy with the sin offerings made by the priests, as in Exodus 29:14).

The principal objection raised by the eighteenth-century explorers was that the Church of the Holy Sepulchre is located *within* the walls of the Old City. Subsequent archaeology has shown that two thousand years ago the tomb over which the church now sits would have been *outside* the walls of the city. Jerusalem's walls were expanded northward under King Agrippa I, the grandson of Herod the Great, between AD 41 and 44, thus placing the tomb inside the walls. Therefore, the argument against the location of the tomb in the Church of the Holy Sepulchre on these grounds has lost all force.

Several historical, topographical, and archaeological factors support the belief that the Church of the Holy Sepulchre stands over the tomb in which Jesus was buried. In AD 70, Rome captured and destroyed Jerusalem. In AD 115, Rome once again put down a Jewish revolt, this time largely confined to North Africa. And finally, Rome crushed a third revolt (AD 132–135), led by a man known as Simon Bar Kokhba, or "Son of the Star." In this revolt the city of Jerusalem suffered further destruction.

In response to the third revolt, the Roman emperor Hadrian, who ruled from AD 117 to 138, rebuilt Jerusalem and renamed it Aelia Capitolina. Part of this rebuilding involved intentionally slighting places and edifices that were sacred to Jews and Christians. (It's probable that Hadrian viewed Christianity as a Jewish sect, not a distinct religion.) One place slighted was the empty tomb of Jesus, which Christians had venerated for one century. The tomb was covered over by a large platform on which Hadrian built a temple dedicated to Jupiter and Venus.

Justin Martyr, a native of Palestine, was a contemporary of Simon ben Kosiba and knew firsthand of the high cost of his rebellion. It's not surprising that in his writing he alludes to the recent war and its aftermath: "Christ said among you that he would give the sign of Jonah, exhorting you to repent . . . in order that your nation and city might not be taken and destroyed, as they have been destroyed . . . yet even when your city is captured, and your land ravaged, you do not repent" (108.1, 3).[3]

Justin's reference to "destruction" most likely had in mind the Jewish wars with Rome. His appeal to the words of Jesus, that is, the "sign of the prophet Jonah" (Matthew 12:39), implies that prophecy has been fulfilled. Despite the warning long ago and now the tragic fulfilment, the Jewish people refuse to repent.

In his First Apology written to Marcus Aurelius, Justin refers specifically to Bar Kokhba's persecuting and exterminating Christians:

> [The prophetic books] are also in the possession of all Jews throughout the world; but they, though they read, do not understand what is said, but count us foes and enemies; and, like yourselves, they kill and punish us whenever they have the power, as you can well believe. For in the Jewish war which lately raged, Barchochebas, the leader of the revolt of the Jews, gave orders that Christians alone should be led to cruel punishments, unless they should deny Jesus the Christ and blaspheme. (Justin, 1 Apol. 31.5–6)

Like Justin, Eusebius mentions in his Chronicle the extermination of Christians at the hands of Bar Kokhba: "Cochebas, prince of the Jewish sect, killed the Christians with all kinds of persecutions, [when] they refused to help him against the Roman troops" (Hadrian Year 17). In quashing this rebellion, Romanizing Jerusalem and exterminating Christians, Hadrian inadvertently preserved the most sacred spot in Christianity—the tomb where Jesus was raised to life.

In AD 326–328, Helena, mother of Emperor Constantine (who ruled in AD 306–337), toured the Holy Land. A major part of her mission was to locate sacred sites, especially those associated with Jesus. Locals told her the tomb of Jesus was beneath the Temple of Jupiter and Venus, and she ordered the pagan temple be demolished. Excavation below the surface revealed ancient tombs, apparently confirming the accuracy of the collective memory of the locals. (The idea that locals could recall with accuracy an event or location for two hundred years is not especially remarkable in an ancient setting. Scholars sometimes refer to it as the "continuity of village memory.") Constantine ordered a church to be built over the site. Unfortunately, in laying out the foundation on which the church would rest, all but the lower portion of the tomb was destroyed.

But what about the question of the closeness in location between the tomb of Jesus and the crucifixion? Is it possible Jesus' tomb could have been located around 150 feet northwest of Calvary? Yes. In fact, the affluent Joseph of Arimathea would have enjoyed such a prestigious location near one of the main entry points of the city. John's Gospel agrees: "At the place where Jesus was crucified, there was a garden, and in the garden a new tomb, in which no one had ever been laid. Because it was the Jewish day of Preparation and since the tomb was nearby, they laid Jesus there" (John 19:41–42 NIV).

Archaeology has recently lent support to the Church of the Holy Sepulchre. In 2016 and 2017, the Edicule (pictured on this book cover), a small shrine built over the surviving part of the tomb, was repaired. For the first time in five centuries, the marble cladding that covered the original limestone surface was removed—and experts were given only sixty hours to examine the unsealed sacred tomb. Both the limestone and the debris, which included ceramic, were examined. The most important part was a limestone bench on which the body of Jesus likely lay. Archaeologists found that the remains of the tomb were consistent with the architecture of tombs constructed in Jerusalem in the early first century AD. The bench, or shelf, on which the body of the deceased lay, is an important part of the evidence that supports a first-century date.

I've indicated some of this earlier in the book. Jewish burial practices in the time of Jesus included washing, perfuming, and wrapping the corpse, then placing it on a bench, or shelf, carved into the side of the tomb. Family and friends mourned for seven days, then one year later gathered the bones of the deceased and placed them in a niche or small stone box called an ossuary.

It's likely that the family and friends of Jesus planned to do the same. They washed and wrapped his body and placed it in the tomb that belonged to Joseph of Arimathea. Two women arrived at the tomb early Sunday morning intending to perfume the body of Jesus and, in keeping with Jewish burial tradition, mourn within the tomb itself. In all probability, they and members of Jesus' family planned to gather the bones of Jesus one year later and take them to the family tomb.

Of course, that part of the burial custom did not take place. For when the women arrived at the tomb Sunday morning, they found the stone rolled aside and the tomb empty. Jesus had been raised from the dead, as he had foretold.

12

If the Disciples Invented the Story of Jesus' Resurrection, They Did a Terrible Job

Perhaps the most exciting aspect of historical Jesus resurrection research is its fluidity. There's always more to learn; there's always some new horizon. As we learned in the previous chapter, archaeological discoveries in the Holy Lands (I use the plural "lands" by design) continue to confirm the earliest resurrection accounts.

The Easter event overwhelmed the followers of Jesus to such an extent that it dominated their thought and became the very center of their preaching.[1] Indeed, the message that Jesus himself had proclaimed was subordinated to the proclamation of his resurrection.[2] Yet Jews and pagans alike scoffed at this proclamation, especially so in the second century. So as the title of this chapter says, if the disciples invented the story of Jesus' resurrection, they did a terrible job.

Among the better-known objectors were the previously mentioned Celsus and Porphyry, who ridiculed the Christian proclamation of the resurrection of Jesus on the basis that it rested upon little more than the confused and contradictory testimony of frightened women.[3] Curiously enough, these criticisms potentially lend an important measure of support to the truthfulness of the Easter witness. Before turning to the debate centered on the resurrection of Jesus, let me say a few words about the apologetic role played by the miracles of Jesus.

Early church fathers appealed to the miracles of Jesus as evidence of the truth of his message and the divinity of his person. The early apologist Quadratus (died circa 140), according to church historian Eusebius, claimed,

> The works of our Savior were always present, for they were true, those that were healed, those that were raised from the dead, who were seen not only when they were healed and when they were raised, but were also constantly present, not only while the Savior was on earth, but also after his departure, they remained for quite a while, so that some of them survived even to our day.[4] (*apud* Eusebius, *Historia ecclesiastica* 4.3.2)

That Christians in the second century made much of Jesus' miracles is also witnessed in what late second-century critic Celsus had to say, at least according to Origen (*c.* 185–*c.* 254):

> Celsus . . . represents us as saying that "we deemed him [Jesus] to be the Son of God, because he healed the lame and the blind." (*Contra Celsum* 2.48)

Many other ancient Christian testimonies point to the miracles of Jesus as proof of his divinity and the truth of his teaching. Origen wrote that reports of miracles, including raising the dead, are "not something made up."[5] He also wrote: "We must observe also that the stupendous acts of [Christ's] power were able to bring to faith those of Christ's own time" (*Commentarii in evangelium Joannis* 2.34[28]).

In short, the miracles prove that Jesus truly is the Son of God and the Savior. That Christians reasoned this way comes as no surprise, for an early form of this argument is found on the lips of the Johannine Jesus: "The works that I do in my Father's name bear witness about me" (John 10:25). Jesus said this to his critics and the same to his disciples: "Believe me that I am in the Father and the Father in me; or else believe me for the sake of the works themselves" (John 14:11 rsv). The "works" (for typological and theological reasons called "signs" in the fourth Gospel) bear witness to the heavenly origins of Jesus and to the truth of his message.

There's no question that this miracle-based apologetic helped advance the Christian cause,[6] but its effectiveness was limited by the stiff competition offered by the testimonies and propaganda relating to Asclepius, a widespread and centuries-old healing cult. Its home city was Epidaurus in Greece, but the cult was well represented in many cities in the eastern Roman Empire, possibly in Israel itself.[7]

Not only are numerous stories of healing recounted in late antique literature, but there's impressive archaeological evidence, including stone and metal figurines representing what body parts had been healed and countless testimonials inscribed in stone.[8] And it wasn't the Asclepius cult alone; there were healing cults linked to other gods and goddesses as well. The miracles of Jesus were impressive, and the continuing miracles that took place "in his name" were impressive, but in a strict sense they were not unique and so their apologetic value was limited.

What trumped Asclepius and others was the resurrection of Jesus, for no Greco-Roman cult promised resurrection. How could they have? After all, as Apollo, son of Zeus, admits, "[Resurrection] is a thing for which my father never made curative spells" (Aeschylus, *Eumenides* 649–650). This is why Aeschylus is forced to confess, "When the dust has soaked up a man's blood, once he is dead, there is no resurrection" (Aeschylus, *Eumenides* 647–648). Consistent with this view, Iamblichus asserts that the soul "goes forth from the body, and upon going forth is separated and scattered" (*apud* Stobaeus, *Eclogae* 1). The implication is that the separated, scattered soul will never be reassembled and will never live again. Asclepius might be able to heal this or that ailment, but he could not offer life beyond the grave. The resurrection of Jesus was the game changer. Nothing could compete with that. But was this remarkable claim true?

A number of years ago, Russ Dudrey observed that in all probability authors of fictional accounts of the resurrection of Jesus would have told the story differently from the way it's told in the canonical Gospels. He rightly noted that their accounts are vulnerable to several objections and criticisms, criticisms that are in fact raised in Jewish and pagan circles.[9] In response to pagan objectors, second-century Christian writers revised and embellished the Gospel accounts. In other words, they wrote the narratives the way they "should have been written" in the first place, had the production of convincing accounts—rather than the awkward, sometimes embarrassing truth—been the objective of the Gospel writers.

The failure to write the accounts this way, reasons Dudrey, is evidence of the antiquity and probable truth of the accounts: "If one presumes that the Gospel writers were 'Christ conspirators' fabricating Christian fiction by inventing the story of the resurrection, then surely they should have done a better job of it."[10] In a sense, then, the criticisms of critics like Celsus and Porphyry unwittingly support the truthfulness of the earliest accounts of the resurrection of Jesus.

In recent work, I've been able to elaborate on the principal point of Dudrey's argument and to extend it further.[11] I shall argue my case by appealing to the criticisms of Celsus and Porphyry and how second-century writings, such as the Gospel of Peter and the Acts of Pilate, respond to these criticisms. These writings serve as exemplars of how some Christians embellished the canonical resurrection accounts for apologetic purposes, so that—to build on Dudrey's point—the story is told the way the objectors thought it should be if it is to be convincing.

Celsus

Sometime in AD 175–181, the pagan philosopher Celsus wrote a hard-hitting critique of Christian faith titled *The True Doctrine*, a work that exists only in Origen's third-century response titled *Contra Celsum*.[12] Robert Wilken sums up the essence of Celsus's polemic: The "early Christians cannot produce reliable witnesses to the events they claim took place."[13] After all, an extraordinary event of this nature requires compelling testimony if it is to be believed. Celsus, however, finds fault with the story of Jesus' death and resurrection at almost every point.

Celsus sees Jesus as a coward whose prayer in Gethsemane portrays him fearfully begging for his life: "Why does he cry: 'Father, if only this cup could pass by me!' A fine God indeed who fears what he is supposed to conquer."[14] This cowardice of Jesus, he said, is the primary reason Jesus' own disciples fled from him at the arrest and crucifixion, did not believe him, and betrayed him: "Your case is made the harder because not even his disciples believed him at the time of his humiliation."[15] Jesus' lack of fortitude and heroism when facing the cross is the main reason for the disciples' disbelief: "Would a god—a saviour, as you say, and son of the Most High God—be betrayed by the very men who had been taught by him and shared everything with him? What an absurdity."[16] Even Jesus' own followers, he says, did not believe in him until they manufactured the story of his abandonment of the grave:

> Have you forgotten that while he lived this Jesus convinced nobody—not even his own disciples—of his divinity, and was punished shamefully for his blasphemies? Were he a god he should not have died, if only to convince other for good and all that he was no liar; but die he did—not only that, but died a death that can hardly be accounted an example to men.[17]

It was against this kind of criticism that the Gospel of Peter, probably composed sometime in the middle of the second century, responded.[18] The strategy of Peter, judging by what survives of this work,[19] is to further the incipient apologetic in the Gospel of Matthew, which, unlike the books of Mark and Luke, has introduced a guard at the tomb (Matthew 27:62–66; 28:4, 11–15).[20] I will briefly comment on what I think are the most relevant passages.

First, the Gospel of Peter provides an explanation for the disciples' fear and desertion of Jesus: "But I with my companions was grieved, and being wounded in mind we hid. For we were being sought by them as evildoers and as those wishing to burn the temple. But through all of these things we were fasting and were sitting, mourning and weeping night and day until the Sabbath" (Akhmîm fragment 7:26–27). The disciples were forced into hiding, not because of cowardice but because of a false and dangerous allegation in which they were accused of plotting to "burn the temple." Moreover, the disciples are portrayed as piously fasting with deep emotions awaiting the Sabbath morn. Therefore, according to the Gospel of Peter, the disciples found it necessary to hide because their lives were threatened, not because of unbelief or doubts about their master.[21] They did not, says Léon Vaganay, "flee as cowards."[22]

Given these problems, Celsus concludes, "No wise man believes the gospel."[23] But there are more problems with the Christian story about Jesus. If Jesus were God, reasons Celsus, he would have appeared to the illustrious and educated men of the empire. Indeed, Jesus should have appeared to his Jewish and Roman enemies, not simply to peasant folk. Moreover, the Christian notion of resurrection is anti-intellectual, irrational, and contrary to philosophy. The default Christian response to critical debate and questioning is, according to Celsus, "Do not ask questions; just believe."[24] Dudrey puts the criticism of Celsus into context: "This is not mere intellectual snobbery on Celsus's part: the social dynamics of the Greco-Roman world were dominated by questions of status and public dignity. Jesus had none, and neither did his followers."[25]

In what appears to be an attempt to respond to these apparent defects in the gospel story, the Gospel of Peter confirms the resurrection of Jesus with a Roman governor and centurion, Petronius, who refers to Jesus as the "Son of God" (Akhmîm fragment 11:45–46). The author asserts that the first witnesses of Jesus' resurrection are Romans—officials, no less!

This is what Celsus expected. Even more, Pilate's responsibility for the death of Jesus is mitigated. In the Gospel of Peter, the Roman governor says, "I am clean from the blood of the son of God." He says this after the Jewish leaders, having only moments earlier witnessed a vindicated Jesus, possessing a supernatural body whose height surpassed the clouds (Akhmîm fragment 10:40), asked Pilate to order his Roman security detachment to lie about witnessing the resurrection of Jesus: "Therefore, Pilate ordered the centurion and the soldiers to say nothing" (Akhmîm fragment 11:49).

It's important to note that Matthew's earlier story, in which the soldiers were ordered to spread the story that the disciples stole the body of Jesus while the guards slept (Matthew 28:11–15), has been dropped. The guards could hardly serve as credible witnesses if they had been asleep. In the Acts of Pilate (c. AD 160), the guards remain fully conscious and attentive when the angel of the Lord descends. They witness—and therefore confirm—what the canonical evangelists relate. The guards in the Acts of Pilate version tell the ruling priests,

> We saw an angel descend from heaven, and he rolled away the stone from the mouth of the cave, and sat upon it, and he shone like snow and like lightning. And we were in great fear, and lay like dead men. And we heard the voice of the angel speaking to the women who waited at the tomb: "Do not be afraid. I know that you seek Jesus who was crucified. He is not here. He has risen, as he said. Come and see the place where the Lord lay. And go quickly and tell his disciples that he has risen from the dead and is in Galilee." (Acts of Pilate 13:1)

The New Testament Gospels have no resurrection witnesses of this caliber. For this reason, Celsus taunts the early Christian movement for its puerile attempt to convince the world of Jesus' resurrection, yet without providing credible eyewitnesses. No belief is more devious, full of contradictions, and open to criticism, says Celsus, than the report of Jesus' resurrection. For Celsus, differences in the canonical accounts meant contradictions. The only witnesses to the alleged resurrection, says Celsus, are hysterical and deluded:

> But who really saw [the resurrection]? A hysterical woman, as you admit and perhaps one other person—both deluded by his sorcery, or else so wrenched with grief at his failure that they hallucinated him risen from the dead by a sort of wishful thinking. . . . If this Jesus were trying to convince anyone of his powers, then surely he ought to have appeared first to the Jews who treated him so badly—and to his accusers—indeed to everyone, everywhere. Or better, he might have saved himself the trouble of getting buried and simply have disappeared from the cross. Has

there ever been such an incompetent planner: When he was in the body, he was disbelieved but preached to everyone; after his resurrection, apparently wanting to establish a strong faith, he chooses to show himself to one woman and a few comrades only. When he was punished, everyone saw; yet risen from the tomb, almost no one. . . . This is not my own guessing: I base what I say on your own writings, which are self-refuting. What god has ever lived among men who offers disbelief as the proof of his divinity? What god appears in turn only to those who already look for his appearances, and is not even recognized by them?[26]

The Gospel of Peter seems to respond to this very complaint. According to the fragment, the resurrection was observed by Roman guards and the very Jewish leaders who had condemned Jesus to death (9:35–11:45). And so the report of the empty tomb and resurrection no longer rests upon a "hysterical woman . . . and perhaps one other person," as Celsus puts it. On the contrary, Jesus did appear "first to the Jews who treated him so badly—and to his accusers"! This is not to say that the Gospel of Peter was specifically composed as an answer to Celsus, but it does seem to reflect an apologetic retelling of the burial and resurrection of Jesus with the kind of criticism seen in Celsus's mind, and which was circulating in the second century.[27]

By providing credible witnesses, the Gospel of Peter fragment eliminates grounds for the kind of doubt put forward by skeptics like Celsus.[28] The author of the Gospel of Peter emphasizes that many eyes "kept watch" on Jesus' tomb after "they spread out seven seals" (Akhmîm fragment 8:33). Tobias Nicklas has noted how striking it is that the Gospel of Peter underscores "sensual perception," in that the soldiers, centurion, and Jewish elders "see" and "hear" what takes place during the resurrection of Jesus:[29]

Gospel of Peter 9:36: "and they *saw*"
10:38: "and so those soldiers *having seen*"

39a: "what they *had seen*"

39b: "again they *see*"

41: "And they were *hearing*"

42: "was *heard*"

The Gospel of Peter takes care to show that it was not possible for the disciples to remove the body of Jesus from the tomb (as was rumored in Matthew 28:11–15). The Jewish leaders were not in a hurry to leave the place of burial; instead, they were "pitching a tent there" (Akhmîm fragment 8:33). The Gospel of Peter further accentuates the Matthean apologetic by showing there is no way the disciples could have stolen the body. The disciples, having fled, were fasting; meanwhile the tomb of Jesus was constantly under observation, making it impossible for the disciples (or for any other grave robbers) to remove the body of Jesus, as was rumored in Matthew 28:11–15.

The polemics of Celsus seems to represent the skeptical climate circulating in the second century, which was likely known to the author of the Gospel of Peter.[30] The Gospel of Peter is in part an apologetic reaction to pagan criticism, such as we see in *Celsus*, specifically in reference to credibility of the resurrection story. The Gospel of Peter and the Acts of Pilate exemplify an apologetic that addresses second-century Jewish and pagan criticisms of the resurrection narratives of the older New Testament Gospels. The resurrection narrative of the Gospel of Peter is also unique, for the New Testament Gospels say nothing about humans—followers or non-followers—observing the resurrection of Jesus.

Porphyry

Porphyry (c. AD 232–303) was a native of Tyre. In his youth he heard Origen preach. He studied Hebrew Scripture, especially the Gospels, but found them lacking in literary quality and philosophical sophistication.[31] Porphyry was eighteen when the persecution broke out under Emperor Decius (r. 249–251). Although at one time sympathetic toward Jesus and the Christian movement, he later developed an intense hatred for religion. Like modern-day "new atheists," Porphyry came to regard Christianity as the most pernicious form of disease infecting the empire. His fifteen-book *Against the Christians* is preserved in part in the writings of Eusebius and Apollinarius, and especially in the *Apocriticus* composed by Marcarius Magnes in the fourth or fifth century.[32] Porphyry echoes several of Celsus's criticisms of Christian beliefs.

Like Celsus, Porphyry claims that the Gospels' portraits of the death of Jesus are absurd and not based on credible eyewitnesses, as seen by their apparent contradictions and the lack of firsthand reports. He says,

> The evangelists were fiction writers—not observers or eyewitnesses to the life of Jesus. Each of the four contradicts the other in writing his account[[33]] of the events and of his suffering and crucifixion. . . . Based on these contradictory and second-hand reports, one might think this describes not the suffering of a single individual but of several! Where one says, "Into your hands I will deliver my spirit," another says, "It is finished" and another "My God, my God, why have you forsaken me," and another "My God, my God why do you punish me." (*Apocrit.* 2.12)[34]

The Gospel of Peter counters this sort of criticism by claiming that the first witnesses of Jesus' resurrection were a Roman centurion and his soldiers, along with hostile Jewish elders and scribes, whose testimony can hardly be doubted. Porphyry sees the account of the passion and resurrection of Jesus as a "legend lifted from accounts of several crucifixions" and asks why Jesus did not stare down his enemies after his resurrection. Again, the Gospel of Peter rebuts the criticism, describing a Jesus who is tall enough to be seen by all and is more than enough to stare down anyone. The impression one receives from the canonical Gospels is that Jesus appears only to the lowly of his day, persons with little social standing and little credibility.

The pagan's demand for a worthy witness is a protest against witnesses who have no credibility. Instead of appearing to credible persons, says Porphyry, Jesus "appeared to Mary Magdalene, a prostitute who came from some horrible little village and had been possessed by seven demons, and another Mary, equally known, probably a peasant woman, and others who were of no account" (*Apocrit.* 2.14).[35] Accordingly, Porphyry asks, "[W]hy did this Jesus not appear to Pilate . . . or to the king of the Jews, Herod, or to the high priest of the Jewish people, or to many men at the same time"? (*Apocrit.* 2.14). As we have seen, according to the Gospel of Peter, that is exactly what the risen Jesus did: He appeared to Jewish people of the highest rank and to the Roman guards who reported all to Pilate.

The chronology of the appearance tradition is cast in a new way in the Gospel of Peter. Only after the Jewish and Roman leaders have seen the resurrected "son of God," do the women fearfully venture to the tomb (Akhmîm fragment 12:50–52). The narrator again reminds his audience that the stone was "great" (Akhmîm fragment 12:54) and the women were concerned about moving the stone, fearful the Jews would see them visiting, and decided to mourn when they returned home (Akhmîm fragment 12:52–54).

The resurrection is mocked and attacked by other thinkers from late antiquity, whose views can be found in the writings of several Fathers of the Church (see Gregory of Nyssa, *Oratio catechetica* 5; Lactantius, *Divinarum institutionum libri* 4.16, 5.2; and Libanius, *Orationes* 18.178; see also the pagan perspective in Lucian, *De morte Peregrini* 11). Romans viewed the Christian message of resurrection as strange, even disgusting. The New Testament itself attests this Greco-Roman aversion to resurrection belief. As I mentioned earlier, we see this among

Christians themselves in Corinth, perhaps influenced by the Platonic notion of the soul, who apparently believed there was no literal resurrection (1 Corinthians 15:12). We may see it also in the reference to Hymanaeus and Philetus, men who either denied or spiritualized the resurrection by declaring that it had already occurred (2 Timothy 2:18). Of course, pagan skepticism is clearly in evidence in Athens when Paul was "mocked" on Mars Hill for proclaiming the resurrection (Acts 17:32).

The New Testament Gospel resurrection narratives are not easily harmonized, thus making it easy for skeptics to attack them. Only Matthew's tradition mentions the guard at the tomb and the seal on the burial stone. Only Lukan tradition narrates Jesus' appearance to the two disciples on the way to Emmaus (Luke 24:13–25). Only the Johannine tradition mentions Nicodemus's involvement in the burial of Jesus, Jesus' appearance to Mary Magdalene (John 20:1, 11–18), Peter and John's run to the empty tomb (John 20:3–10), Thomas's challenge that unless he met the risen Christ he would not believe (John 20:24–29), the disciples going back to their previous vocation as fishermen (John 21:4–6), and Peter's restoration over Jesus' breakfast (John 21:7–19). If all these things really happened, why are they not mentioned in the Synoptic Gospels?

Of course, there are differences in the canonical resurrection accounts, and some are not so easily reconciled. For critics like Celsus and Porphyry, differences meant contradictions that were irreconcilable. The tradition contains a number of discrepancies in incidental details, which left the canonical narratives vulnerable to attack:

1. Which women visited the tomb on Easter morning? The Markan tradition reports three women: Mary Magdalene, Mary the mother of James, and Salome (Mark 16:1). The Matthean tradition speaks of two women, Mary Magdalene and the "other" Mary (Matthew

28:1). The Lukan tradition portrays at least five women—two Marys and Joana—and adds "the other women" without any more specificity (Luke 24:1, 10).

2. The canonical tradition does not agree with regard to the angels announcing the resurrection: Mark tells of a "young man" (Mark 16:5), while Luke mentions two dazzling men (Luke 24:4); Matthew, like Mark, has one "angel of the Lord" at the resurrection tomb without mentioning a youthfulness (Matthew 28:2–3), and the Johannine narrative omits the angel(s) altogether.

3. There is some geographical confusion regarding the location of the resurrection appearances: Were they in Galilee or in Jerusalem? The Markan tradition (rightly omitting 16:9–20) has no appearances; the text in its current form does not fulfil Jesus' most important Markan prediction of resurrection. In Mark 16:7, the disciples are told that Jesus will meet them in Galilee. The Luke-Acts narrative appearances occur exclusively around Jerusalem (Luke 24:36–41; Acts 1:6–11). The Matthean and Johannine tradition present Jesus' post-mortem appearances in Jerusalem and Galilee (Matthew 28:1–10, 16; John 20–21).

In his polemical work *Contra Galilaeos*, Julian "the Apostate" points out several contradictions in the synoptic resurrection accounts.[36] According to Cyril, Julian

wrote that the holy evangelists contradict themselves when they say: Mary Magdalene and the other Mary (following Matthew 28:11), late on the Sabbath when the first of the week began to dawn, came to the tomb; according to Mark [16:2], however, after it began to be daylight and the sun had risen. And according to Matthew they saw an angel [28:2]; according to Mark a young man [16:5]; and according to Matthew they left and told the disciples about the resurrection of Christ [28:8]—according to Mark they were silent and told no one anything [16:8]. By means of these things he brings censure on the holy scriptures and says that they contradict each other.[37]

The canonical traditions give no eyewitnesses of the resurrection event itself, only of the discovery of the empty tomb, the presence of one or more angels, and the appearances of Jesus. In the Matthean account, Roman soldiers observe an angel descending from heaven, who rolls away the stone and sits upon it. We have the tomb opening, soldiers observing, and an empty tomb; however, nobody sees Jesus rise from the dead. According to the Synoptic tradition, we're left wondering where Jesus is: "Why . . . seek the living among the dead? He is not here, but has risen" (Luke 24:5–6; see slightly different wording in Mark 16:6 and Matthew 28:6). This is exactly the gap the Gospel of Peter seems to fill.

Despite the fact that the enemies of Jesus knew of the resurrection, only Jesus' allies are witnesses of the empty tomb. Initially we're told of at least five women; later we hear of Peter and John visiting the empty tomb. We're dependent on the later Johannine tradition for a male account of an empty tomb, that of Peter and John (John 20:1–10). Mark and Matthew do not reflect this tradition, and Lukan tradition provides limited detail of Peter's visit to the tomb (Luke 24:12). Other than Peter, as described in Luke 24:12, and Peter and John in the Johannine narrative (John 20:1–10), the earliest witnesses of Jesus' resurrection are women, who in late antiquity were viewed as dubious witnesses.

Why do all the followers of Jesus, except John, who "saw and believed" (John 20:8–9), expect to find Jesus' corpse in the tomb? The Johannine tradition presents the disciples wondering if grave robbers have stolen him away (John 20:2, 13–15). When the risen Jesus appears in the upper room, the apostles are chastised for unbelief and hardness of heart because they did not believe the women's report that he had risen (Luke 24:11, 13–35).

The Gospel of Peter's recasting of the resurrection story addresses the perceived problems in the earlier canonical Gospels. This second-century writing attempts to rebut pagan criticism by providing eyewitnesses (hostile ones, at that), who possess much more credibility than women, *of the resurrection event itself.* These witnesses are Roman guards and Jewish elders, who see angelic beings enter the tomb and lead a transformed, vindicated Jesus out of the tomb.[38]

The disciples' fear and flight are explained. The chronology of postmortem events is transposed in the second-century context to answer skepticism of Jesus' resurrection. Only after the social elite, the power brokers of Jewish Palestine, have experienced the resurrected Jesus do the women and disciples witness the empty tomb. Thus, the resurrection testimony of the followers of Jesus is subordinated to that of Jesus' enemies. Pontius Pilate, who had been unwilling to crucify Jesus, is exonerated, and the blame is shifted to Herod and Jewish leaders. Our analysis has enabled us to see some significant points of cultural, political, and social coherence between apologetic elements in the Gospel of Peter and second-century pagan skepticism.[39]

The Gospel of Peter also seems to bear witness to an unanticipated effect the story of the risen Jesus had on late antique Greco-Roman literary culture. While critics like Celsus devised arguments against the plausibility of the Christian story, novelists drew inspiration from it. Some twenty-five years ago, classicist Glen Bowersock raised the interesting possibility that the Gospels' story of the death, burial, and discovery of the empty tomb gave rise to the theme of *Scheintod*, "apparent death," which appeared in the novels of several Greco-Roman authors within one century or so of the circulation of the Christian

Gospels.[40] We find probable examples in *Chaereas and Callirhoe* by Chariton (late first or early second century), *Leucippe and Clitophon* by Achilles Tatius (late second century), and the *Ephesian Tale* by Xenophon of Ephesus (late second or early third century). Even the *Life of Apollonius* by Philostratus (third century) may have been influenced by the Christian Gospels.[41]

In these lurid accounts of kidnapping, apparent murder, and miraculous escapes, we hear of empty tombs, stones moved aside, missing bodies, everyone in town running to the grave, and speculations about revivification, ascension to heaven, and even apotheosis, Christ's elevation to divine status. In one of these novels, we almost certainly have an allusion to the words of institution.[42] In view of these literary interests and developments in the second century, Bowersock plausibly suggests that Celsus's objections to the Christian proclamation of the resurrection of Jesus make good sense. Celsus is reacting not simply to the original proclamation, the way the story was told in the middle of the first century, but to the impact the story was having in his time, in the middle of the second century. It's against this backdrop that his critical questioning makes good sense: "We must examine this question, whether anyone who really died ever rose again with the same body" (Origen, *Contra Celsum* 2.55).[43] In their own playful ways, this is the very question that underlies the interest in *Scheintod* we see in the Greek romances.

It seems, then, that the accounts of the first-century Christian Gospels gave rise to new ideas exploited and exaggerated in late-first and second-century Greek novels, which in turn influenced, perhaps even led to, the creation of second-century works such as the Acts of Paul and Thecla, Acts of John, and other writings customarily regarded by scholars as "apocryphal" but which are probably better regarded as Christian novels.

I think we should regard the Akhmîm gospel fragment as one more second-century Christian writing, or novel, that reflects a number of the features we see in the secular romances and in the just-mentioned fictional books of Acts.[44] Like the Greek romances that have been reviewed, the Akhmîm gospel fragment tells an exciting tale of the execution and burial of Jesus, complete with elaborate precautions to see to it that no resurrection story results. But the resurrection does happen, in full view of a crowd of hostile eyewitnesses. The stone that covered the entrance to the tomb is—by itself—moved aside. Two men who descended from heaven enter the tomb and lead Jesus out of it. The heads of all three reach up to the very heavens themselves. A voice from heaven is heard, and the cross on which Jesus had been crucified answers back.

The Jewish and Roman witnesses are astounded and report all to the governor, who now regrets what he allowed to happen and declares that he is innocent, declaring that the death of Jesus was "all your doing!" (11.46). The Jewish leaders surround the governor and beg him to keep from the public what has happened. After all, "It is better to make ourselves guilty of a great sin before God, and not fall into the hands of the people of the Jews and be stoned" (11.48). As does the governor in Xenophon's novel, so the governor in the gospel fragment changes his mind, regretting what he has done.

What the gospel story of the death, burial, and resurrection of Jesus inspired in the Greco-Roman novels, the latter, in turn, appear to have inspired the Gospel of Peter, the Acts of Pilate, and a number of other apocryphal books of Acts and accounts of martyrdom. The ancient Passion stories of the early church generated imaginative fiction in both pagan and Christian settings, as all attempted to compose ever more exciting narratives. The Gospel of Peter is part of this interesting development, in which its author attempts to expand the apologetic of the Gospel of Matthew, so as to counter mocking criticisms and defend the truth of the resurrection of Jesus, and in which at the same time the author reflects the crass literary devices of what in his day was hardly more than pulp fiction.

Why This Review Matters

The extra-canonical Gospel of Peter and the Acts of Pilate provide us a number of examples of how accounts of the resurrection could have and should have been written had the goal been a compelling and convincing story but not a factual one.

In contrast, the canonical Gospels present restrained, sober narrative. Their accounts exhibit a commitment to veracity and not to apologetically driven embellishment and excess. They leave their stories open to criticism, even an apparent vulnerability, because of a commitment to the ancient sources and traditions. Of course, the Gospels were not written in a way that anticipated second-century skeptics.

The Gospel of Peter and the Acts of Pilate, however, illustrate perfectly the kind of creative, expansive embellishment that the evangelists "should have done" if they had attempted to fabricate a more convincing account of the resurrection of Jesus.

Careful comparison of the dissimilarities of the resurrection accounts from the first century and the second century with pagan criticism of the second century helps us appreciate more the candor and commitment to truth we see on the part of the first-century Gospel writers, which cogently show us the reliability of the resurrection accounts embedded in the Gospel narratives.

From Oxford to Jerusalem—My Academic Journey

Whether you are a scholar, are planning scholarly work, or don't see scholarly work, per se, in your future, you might be interested in knowing more about my personal academic journey—especially as it pertains *Body of Proof*.

Written for skeptics, seekers, and followers of Jesus alike, this book, which requires little to no prerequisite knowledge of Christianity or scholarly systems, stands squarely on the shoulders of more than a dozen years of intense research, scholarly meetings, academic roundtables, and learned conferences. Research began residentially in Oxford and the truly phenomenal Bodleian library system there.

My studies required me to present academic papers at learned meetings and examine ancient texts (papyri, codices, and the like) at the renowned Griffith Papyrology Room in Oxford's Sackler Library. By God's grace, our young family lived across the street from the Sackler, which allowed me to wear out my library welcome. My quest to learn more took me to the University of Edinburgh (with Professor Paul Foster), the University of Manchester's John Rylands Library, the Beinecke Rare Book and Manuscript Library of Yale University, and the Shrine of the Book in Jerusalem.

Academically speaking, I had to gain facility in Christian origins, Jesus and the Gospels, and topics, especially apologetics, that closely related to Jesus and the Gospels. These include the resurrection of Jesus, New Testament manuscripts (their number, nature, and reliability), extracanonical gospels, resurrection, and afterlife beliefs.

During my doctoral residency at Oxford, I made it my personal ambition to invest as much time as I could studying the oldest and most valuable manuscripts of the Bible. I have had the enriching and humbling experience of holding the oldest, most priceless biblical fragments and manuscripts with my own hands. Professor Evans surprised me when he said he thought I had held more biblical manuscripts in my hands than 90 percent of Bible scholars. I am in love with the Word of God. Each fragment has a story of discovery and preservation.

There were comical moments along the way. After all, we can't take ourselves too seriously when doing academic research. At the Society of Biblical Literature (SBL) annual meeting in Chicago, in 2012, I was the only "non-Craig" to present a paper, followed by discussion on the resurrection of Jesus. The theme was "External Confirmations of New Testament History." Craig Hazen presided, and Craig Evans, Craig Keener, Craig Blomberg, William Lane Craig, and I presented. I will never forget Craig Keener encouraging me to carry on in my studies because of some new and exciting arguments for the resurrection of Jesus I was researching, which years later are now offered in this book.

You never forget the first time you're cited by another scholar in a peer-reviewed publication. A year or so later, in German scholarship, I was surprised to see that Thomas J. Kraus interacted with my resurrection research a couple of times in *Early*

Christianity 3, published in 2013. My research and contribution to knowledge of Jesus' physical resurrection would go on to be published in a respected academic monograph series—*Jewish and Christian Texts*—published by Bloomsbury T & T Clark, edited by Professor James H. Charlesworth of Princeton Theological Seminary. Professor Charlesworth wrote the following in the editor's preface to my monograph:

> I am pleased to publish Jeremiah J. Johnston's careful and erudite study of Jesus' resurrection. . . . This stunning composition helps us comprehend the long historical process of debating and vetting what will be called "the New Testament." . . . Dr. Johnston's learned work makes a significant contribution to a field of study that a growing number of scholars now view as mainstream New Testament research.[1]

Professor Evans added his scholarly voice in support of my research in the academic monograph's foreword: "It is for these reasons that I am so pleased to see the publication of Dr. Jeremiah Johnston's dissertation. His research makes a vital contribution." I wish to express my gratitude to Craig Evans for inspiring me with the idea to pursue this study, and after all, I moved into his home library for six weeks in Nova Scotia, Canada, to complete the original thesis work. Professor Evans is the consummate scholar, and I have learned so much from him that words could never convey my love and appreciation for who he is.

Complete List of Book Publications

- *Unleashing Peace: Experiencing God's Shalom in Your Pursuit of Happiness*
- *Scribes and Their Remains*, editor, with Craig A. Evans (*Studies in Scripture in Early Judaism and Christianity* 21/LSTS 94)

- *Answers to Tough Questions: Defending What You Believe*
- *Unimaginable: What Our World Would Be Like Without Christianity*
- *The Dark Side* (a leader's kit, DVDs, and a study book)
- *The Resurrection of Jesus in the Gospel of Peter: A Tradition-Historical Study of the Akhmîm Gospel Fragment*, with Craig A. Evans (*Jewish and Christian Texts in Contexts and Related Studies*)
- *Unanswered: Lasting Truth for Trending Questions* (book, Bible study book, personal Bible study book, and teaching video series)
- *Searching the Scriptures: Studies in Context and Intertextuality*, editor, with Craig A. Evans (*Studies in Scripture in Early Judaism and Christianity* 19; LNTS 543; SSEJC 19)

Notes

Introduction

1. "Resurrection did not happen, say quarter of Christians," BBC News, April 9, 2017, https://www.bbc.com/news/uk-england-39153121; BBC—Religion and Ethics Polling, http://comresglobal.com/wp-content/uploads/2017/04/BBC-Religion-and-Ethics-Survey-Data-Tables-1.pdf.

2. For the skeptically minded: Following the completion of my PhD, I have published approximately 150,000 words on the history and evidential basis for Jesus' bodily resurrection from the dead in an academic monograph, peer-reviewed journals, serials, and reference works. These include substantial entries in Oxford University Press reference works and edited volumes published by E. J. Brill and Mohr Siebeck. In my doctoral program, the Lord blessed me to work closely under the supervision of Professor Craig A. Evans (Houston Baptist University) and Professor Paul Foster (University of Edinburgh) in concert with extremely helpful recommendations offered by my external examiner, Professor William Telford (Durham University). You can read more about my personal academic journey at the end of this book.

Chapter 1 "Isn't the Resurrection Imaginative Storytelling?"

1. Sam Roberts, "Jesus of Nazareth, Whose Messianic Message Captivated Thousands, Dies at About 33," March 25, 2016, *Vanity Fair*. Printed with permission. Contributors: Reza Aslan, Markus Bockmuehl, Raymond E. Brown, Gordon Campbell, Bart D. Ehrman, Jeremiah J. Johnston, Philip J. King, Helmut Koester, Tim Laniak, Daniel Master, Lawrence E. Stager, Cary L. Summers, and Peter Williams; https://www.vanityfair.com/culture/2016/03/jesus-new-york-times-obituary.

2. The main difference is that, in the case of most of the emperors (probably all), we have extant correspondence to them and from them that is genuine and so dates to their time in office. We also have official government documents that announce their decrees or other matters, and again, these are genuine. Thanks to the papyri found in Egypt, we actually have autographs of officials discussing imperial business, decisions of emperors, and so on. We have nothing like this with regard to Jesus. Jesus wrote nothing, and nothing was written to him. Also, statues and inscriptions in honor of the emperors were erected during their respective reigns. That cannot be said of Jesus. However, discussion of Jesus, by his first followers and then later followers (say, the first three hundred years) approximates and in some cases exceeds that of most of the Roman emperors. Nothing like this can be said for a non-emperor person in the Roman empire.

3. Dr. Jack Graham, "Men Who Win" sermon, June 19, 2022, Prestonwood Baptist Church, Plano, Texas.

Chapter 2 The Case against Jesus' Resurrection

1. E. P. Sanders, *The Historical Figure of Jesus* (London: Penguin, 1993), 11, 13.

Chapter 3 The Christian Claim That Jesus Was Resurrected

1. Jeremiah J. Johnston, *Unanswered: Lasting Truth for Trending Questions* (New Kensington, PA: Whitaker House, 2015), 63–64. Following the rights to *Unanswered* returned to me, this excerpt and others have been slightly edited to best fit *Body of Proof*.

2. *Antiquities* 18:117–119.

3. *Jewish Wars [J.W.]* 2.163.

4. *Jewish Wars [J.W.]* 2.154–55.

5. Dead Sea Scrolls, (4Q521 frag. 2, col. 2, line 12).

6. For detailed discussion of Jesus' kingdom proclamation, see Jeremiah J. Johnston and C. A. Evans, "Kingdom of God/Heaven," in *The Oxford Encyclopedia of Bible and Theology*, edited by Samuel E. Balentine et al. (Oxford and New York: Oxford University Press, 2014); Jeremiah J. Johnston and C. A. Evans, "Kingdom of God," in *Encyclopedia of Early Christianity*, edited by Paul J.J. van Geest, Bert Jan Lietaert Peerbolte, David Hunter (Leiden: Brill, 2015).

7. For discussion of Mark 12:18–27, see R. T. France, *The Gospel of Mark* (NIGTC; Grand Rapids: Eerdmans; Carlisle: Paternoster, 2002), 469–75; for Matthew 22:23–33, see John Nolland, *The Gospel of Matthew* (NIGTC; Grand Rapids: Eerdmans; Bletchley, UK: Paternoster, 2005), 899–907; for Luke 20:27–40, see Joel B. Green, *The Gospel of Luke* (NICNT; Grand Rapids: Eerdmans, 1997), 717–23.

8. For recent studies of this important exchange, which ably take into account the significance of 4Q521, see Karl-Wilhelm Niebuhr, "Die Werke

des eschatologischen Freudenboten (4Q521 und die Jesusüberlieferung)," in C. M. Tuckett (ed.), *The Scriptures in the Gospels* (BETL 131; Leuven: Peeters and Leuven University Press, 1997), 637–46; Hans Kvalbein, "The Wonders of the End-Time: Metaphoric Language in 4Q521 and the Interpretation of Matthew 11.5 par.," *JSP* 18 (1998): 87–110; Michael Labahn, "The Significance of Signs in Luke 7:22–23 in the Light of Isaiah 61 and the *Messianic Apocalypse*," in C. A. Evans (ed.), *From Prophecy to Testament: The Function of the Old Testament in the New* (Peabody: Hendrickson, 2004), 146–68; Michael Becker, "Der 'messianische Apokalypse' 4Q521 und der Interpretationsrahmen der Taten Jesu," in M. Becker and J. Frey (eds.), *Apokalyptik und Qumran* (Einblicke 10; Paderborn: Bonifatius, 2007), 237–303. In the light of the remarkable parallels between Jesus' reply to John and what we find in 4Q521, it's become evident that the Matthean evangelist rightly recognized the eschatological and messianic import of both John's question and Jesus' response.

9. Qur'an 4:157–158.

Chapter 4 Reason #1

1. Bill Warner, *The Doctrine of Slavery: An Islamic Institution* (Nashville: CSPI, 2010), 13. Dr. Warner's book should be read for a complete perspective on slavery within Islam and its effect.

2. Warner, *The Doctrine of Slavery*, 30–31.

3. Bill Warner, *Sharia Law for Non-Muslims* (Nashville: CSPI, 2010), 33.

4. For a comprehensive study of the impact of the Jesus movement on history and in modern times, please see my book *Unimaginable: What Our World Would Be Like Without Christianity* (Minneapolis: Bethany House, 2018).

Chapter 5 Reason #2

1. Dan Joseph @danjosephauthor, Twitter, https://twitter.com/danjoseph author/status/1311741733206667266.

2. Jeremiah J. Johnston, *Unanswered*, 65.

3. *Jewish Wars*. 6.5.3 §300–309.

4. *Jewish Wars*. 7.11.1 §437–438; *Life* 76 §424–425.

5. Jeremiah J. Johnston, *The Resurrection of Jesus in the Gospel of Peter* (New York and London: Bloomsbury T & T Clark, 2016), 103.

6. Johnston, *The Resurrection of Jesus in the Gospel of Peter*, 104.

7. For arguments in support of the authenticity of the passion predictions, see Craig A. Evans, "Did Jesus Predict His Death and Resurrection?" in Porter, Hayes, and Tombs (eds.), Resurrection, 82–97. Porter, S. E., M. A. Hayes, and D. Tombs (eds.), Resurrection (JSNTSup 186; RILP 5; Sheffield: Sheffield Academic Press, 1999), 86–96.

8. The expression *Lord's day* appears in the book of Revelation, one of the letters of Ignatius, and the extracanonical Gospel of Peter.

Chapter 6 Reason #3

1. Jeremiah J. Johnston, *Unanswered*, 74–76.

2. According to Zodhiates, of the forty-two times in the New Testament that the word ἀνάστασις occurs, with the exception of Luke 2:34, it always means the resurrection of the body. See Spiros Zodhiates, *The Complete Word Study Dictionary: New Testament* (Chattanooga, TN: AMG Publishers, 1994), see "386. ἀνάστασις."

3. Herod Antipas, seventh son and one of three surviving sons of Herod the Great, was tetrarch of Galilee and Perea (4 BC–AD 39, serving as administrator under Rome. He lost his throne in AD 39 after trying to gain complete sovereignty).

Chapter 8 Reason #5

1. *m. Sanhedrin* 6:5.

2. Semahot 13.7.

3. *m. Sanhedrin* 6:6.

4. J. Magness, "Jesus' Tomb: What Did It Look Like?" in H. Shanks (ed.), *Where Christianity Was Born* (Washington, DC: Biblical Archaeology Society, 2006), 212–26, with quotation from p. 224. Magness is rightly contradicting John Dominic Crossan's claim that the burial of Yehohanan was unusual and that Jesus of Nazareth probably was not buried.

5. Gordon's Tomb in Jerusalem, also known as the Garden Tomb, is a bit misleading because it looks like a tall, rectangular door, similar to other modern doors. This is not, however, the original shape of the Garden Tomb, because an earthquake damaged the tomb entrance. While repairing the entrance, they went ahead and cut the doorway a little higher and made it into what looks like an ordinary door. If you're under six feet tall, you can basically walk straight through. Again, this is for moderns, and it's not the way the tomb was originally constructed. The tomb entrance would have been a square opening.

Chapter 9 Reason #6

1. James D. G. Dunn, *Jesus Remembered*, vol. 1 of *Christianity in the Making* (Grand Rapids: Eerdmans, 2003), 855.

2. Gary R. Habermas, *The Historical Jesus: Ancient Evidence for the Life of Christ* (Joplin: College Press, 1996), 153. See n. 44, which lists the scholars.

3. J. E. Colwell, "Kerygma, Kerygmatic Theology," *New Dictionary of Theology*, 364. The Greek word kērygma is usually translated "proclamation," "preaching" or "announcement," and outside of the New Testament, it was used generally of a public notice proclaimed by a herald whereby that which was announced became effective by the act of announcing it.

4. Dunn, *Jesus Remembered*, 143.

5. Antiquities 20:200 (20.9.1). "When, therefore, Ananus was of this disposition, he thought he had now a proper opportunity [to exercise his authority].

Festus was now dead, and Albinus was but upon the road; so he assembled the sanhedrin of judges, and brought before them the brother of Jesus, who was called Christ, whose name was James, and some others, [or, some of his companions]; and when he had formed an accusation against them as breakers of the law, he delivered them to be stoned"; see Flavius Josephus and William Whiston, *The Works of Josephus: Complete and Unabridged* (Peabody: Hendrickson, 1987), 538.

6. Jeremiah J. Johnston, *Unimaginable: What Our World Would Be Like Without Christianity* (Minneapolis: Bethany House Publishers, 2018).

7. Jeremiah J. Johnston, *Unanswered*, 66.

Chapter 10   Reason #7

1. Walter Isaacson, *Steve Jobs* (New York: Simon & Schuster, 2011), 14–15.

2. C. S. Lewis, *The Collected Letters of C. S. Lewis*, vol. 3, Walter Hooper ed. (New York: HarperCollins, 2004), from a letter to Father Peter Bide dated April 29, 1959.

3. On the meaning of 1 Corinthians 15:29, see Michael F. Hull, *Baptism on Account of the Dead (1 Cor 15:29): An Act of Faith in the Resurrection* (Academia Biblica; Leiden: Brill, 2005).

4. On Christianity's understanding of witness and "martyr," see A. A. Trites, "Μάρτυς and Martyrdom in the Apocalypse: A Semantic Study," *Nov.* 15 (1973): 72–80; idem, "Witness, Testimony," in C. Brown (ed.), *The New International Dictionary of New Testament Theology* (Exeter: Paternoster Press, 1978), 1038–51. Trites rightly cautions against reading later nuances into earlier texts.

5. Dunn, *Jesus Remembered*, 143.

6. From κοιμήθρα, a sleeping place, and κοίμησις, for lying down to sleep.

7. Bernard Green, *Christianity in Ancient Rome: The First Three Centuries* (T&T Clark: London, 2010), 177.

8. Green, *Christianity in Ancient Rome*, 177.

9. Jeremiah J. Johnston, *Unanswered: Lasting Truth for Trending Questions* (New Kensington, PA: Whitaker House, 2015), 76–77. Following the rights to Unanswered returned to me, this excerpt and others have been slightly edited to best fit Body of Proof.

10. F. B. Meyer, Bible.org, https://bible.org/illustration/f-b-meyer.

11. "The Lasting Contributions of a Wretched Worm," Christian History Institute, https://christianhistoryinstitute.org/magazine/article/lasting-contributions-of-a-wretched-worm.

12. Gary Habermas, "My Pilgrimage from Atheism to Theism: An Exclusive Interview with Former British Atheist Professor Antony Flew." Available from the website of Biola University at www.biola.edu/antonyflew. See also David J. Baggett, ed., *Did the Resurrection Happen?: A Conversation with Gary Habermas and Antony Flew* (Downers Grove, IL: InterVarsity Press, 2009), 85.

Chapter 11 The Most Significant Place in Christianity

1. E. Robinson and E. Smith, *Biblical Researches in Palestine*, 3 vols. (London: Murray; Boston: Crocker and Brewster, 1841), 1:407–18. Robinson and Smith visited the Holy Land in 1838. Robinson is well known for identifying an arch on the west side of the Temple Mount ("Robinson's Arch").

2. Gabriel Barkay, "The Garden Tomb: Was Jesus Buried Here?", *Biblical Archaeology Review* 12, no. 2, 1986.

3. Justin Martyr, *Dialogue with Trypho*; Justin Martyr, trans. Thomas B. Falls, *The First Apology, The Second Apology, Dialogue with Trypho, Exhortation to the Greeks, Discourse to the Greeks, The Monarchy or The Rule of God*, vol. 6 of THE FATHERS OF THE CHURCH (Washington, DC: The Catholic University of America Press, 1948), 354.

Chapter 12 If the Disciples Invented the Story of Jesus' Resurrection, They Did a Terrible Job

1. The literature treating the resurrection is enormous: Gerhard Koch, *Die Auferstehung Jesu Christi* (Tübingen: Mohr Siebeck, 1959), 25. For scholarly discussion of resurrection theology and ideas in the New Testament and its environment, see C. F. D. Moule (ed.), *The Significance of the Message of the Resurrection of Jesus Christ* (London: SCM Press, 1968); C. F. Evans, *Resurrection and the New Testament* (SBT 2.12; London: SCM Press, 1970); R. H. Fuller, *The Formation of the Resurrection Narratives* (Philadelphia: Fortress, 1971); Murray J. Harris, *Raised Immortal: Resurrection and Immortality in the New Testament* (Grand Rapids: Eerdmans, 1985); idem, *From Grave to Glory: Resurrection in the New Testament* (Grand Rapids: Zondervan, 1990); Richard N. Longenecker (ed.), *Life in the Face of Death: The Resurrection Message of the New Testament* (Grand Rapids: Eerdmans, 1998); N. T. Wright, *The Resurrection of the Son of God* (Christian Origins and the Question of God 3; Minneapolis: Fortress Press, 2003); Dale C. Allison Jr., *Resurrecting Jesus: The Earliest Christian Tradition and Its Interpreters* (London and New York: T & T Clark International, 2005); Michael R. Licona, *The Resurrection of Jesus: A New Historiographical Approach* (Downers Grove IL: InterVarsity Press, 2010); Christopher Bryan, *The Resurrection of the Messiah* (Oxford: Oxford University Press, 2011).

2. This shift in focus gave rise to the theological debate centered on the problem of how to reckon with the early church's proclamation of the proclaimer.

3. The resurrection is mocked and attacked by other thinkers from late antiquity, whose views can be found in the writings of several Fathers of the Church (see Gregory of Nyssa, *Catechetical Oration* 5; Lactantius, *Institutes* 4.16, 5.2; and Libanius, *Oration* 18.178; see also the pagan perspective in Lucian, *Peregrinus* 11).

4. Translation based on K. Lake, *Eusebius Ecclesiastical History I* (LCL 153; London: Heinemann; Cambridge: Harvard University Press, 1926), 309.

5. The word πλάσμα means something formed or fashioned, often with the connotation of something "faked."

6. To what degree it did is explored in G. W. H. Lampe, "Miracles and Early Christian Apologetic," and Maurice F. Wiley, "Miracles in the Early Church," in C. F. D. Moule (ed.), *Miracles: Cambridge Studies in their Philosophy and History* (London: Mowbray, 1965), 205–18 and 221–34, respectively; Ramsay MacMullen, *Paganism in the Roman Empire* (New Haven and London: Yale University Press, 1981), 94–112; and idem, *Christianizing the Roman Empire (A.D. 100–400)* (New Haven and London: Yale University Press, 1984), 25–42.

7. On the possibility of the presence of the cult of Asclepius in Israel, perhaps in Jerusalem itself, see James H. Charlesworth, *The Good and Evil Serpent* (New Haven: Yale University Press, 2010), 108–16. For a less optimistic view, see Michael Becker, *Wunder und Wundertäten im frührabbinischen Judentum: Studien zum Phänomen und seiner Überlieferung im Horizont von Magie und Dämonismus* (WUNT II. 144; Tübingen: Mohr Siebeck, 2002), 134 n. 208: the evidence for the cult of Asclepius in Jerusalem "can hardly be reconstructed." For a recent study of the cult, see Günther Lorenz, *Asklepios, der Heiler mit dem Hund, und der Orient. Religion und Medizin in alten Kulturen in universalhistorischer Sicht. Gesammelte Schriften* (Innsbruck: Innsbruck University Press, 2016).

8. For a comprehensive collection of Asclepian materials, see Emma J. Edelstein and Ludwig Edelstein, *Asclepius: Collection and Interpretation of the Testimonies* (2 vols., Baltimore and London: The Johns Hopkins University Press, 1945). For critical discussion of the Epidaurian inscriptions, see Lynn R. LiDonnici, *The Epidaurian Miracle Inscriptions: Text, Translation and Commentary* (SBLTT 36; GRR 11; Atlanta: Scholars Press, 1995). That these healing cults competed with one another and were largely motivated by commercial interests was recognized in late antiquity. Christians, too, knew of these interests and criticized the cults accordingly. For an assessment of healing cults, especially the cult of Asclepius, with these practices and motives in mind, see Bernd Manuwald, "Wundergeschichten aus dem Asklepios-Heiligtum von Epidaurus: Dokumente eines religiösen Kommunikationssytems," in Christian Frevel and Henner von Hesberg (eds.), *Kult und Kommunikation: Medien in den Heiligtümern der Antike* (Schriften des Lehr- und Forschungszentrums für die antiken Kulturen des Mittelmeerraumes 4; Wiesbaden: Ludwig Reichert, 2007), 89–120.

9. Russ Dudrey, "What the Writers Should Have Done Better: A Case for the Resurrection of Jesus Based on Ancient Criticisms of the Resurrection Reports," *Stone-Campbell Journal* 3 (2000): 55–78.

10. Dudrey, "What the Writers Should Have Done Better," 57.

11. Jeremiah J. Johnston, *The Resurrection of Jesus in the Gospel of Peter: A Tradition-Historical Study of the Akhmîm Gospel Fragment*, Jewish and Christian Texts in Contexts and Related Studies #21 (New York and London: Bloomsbury T & T Clark, 2016).

12. Origen, *Contra Celsum*, preface 1–4. For the critical edition, see Henry Chadwick, *Origen: Contra Celsum* (Cambridge: Cambridge University, 1953). *On the True Doctrine* has been reconstructed from *Contra Celsum* by R. Joseph Hoffmann, *Celsus on the True Doctrine* (New York: Oxford University Press, 1987). On Celsus, see E. R. Dodds, *Pagan and Christian in an Age of Anxiety* (Cambridge: Cambridge University, 1965), 116–21.

13. Robert L. Wilken, *The Christians as the Romans Saw Them*, 2nd ed. (New Haven: Yale University Press, 2003), 111.

14. R. Joseph Hoffmann, *Celsus on the True Doctrine* (New York: Oxford University Press, 1987), 63–64.

15. Hoffmann, *Celsus on the True Doctrine*, 66.

16. Hoffmann, *Celsus on the True Doctrine*, 61–62.

17. Hoffmann, *Celsus on the True Doctrine*, 65; Origen, *Contra Celsum* 2.21, 39.

18. The criticisms expressed by Celsus likely preceded him by a generation or more.

19. We only have material relating to the trial, burial, and resurrection.

20. For a recent analysis of the Gospel of Peter from this perspective, see Craig A. Evans, "The Gospels of Peter and Thomas," in John J. Collins, Craig A. Evans, and Lee Martin McDonald, *Ancient Jewish and Christian Scriptures: New Developments in Canon Controversy* (Louisville: Westminster John Knox Press, 2020), 167–93, especially 168–82.

21. Rightly observed in Léon Vaganay, *L'Évangile de Pierre* (2nd ed., Paris: Gabalda, 1930), 93: *Dans les deux péricopes . . . Pierre est à l'honneur. Il parle au nom des "Douze" et son discours n'a d'autre but que de justifier la conduite du college apostolique.* ("In the two pericopes . . . Peter is honoured. He speaks in the name of the 'Twelve' and his discourse has no other goal than to justify the leadership of the apostolic assembly.")

22. Vaganay, *comme des lâches*.

23. Hoffmann, *Celsus*, 75; Origen, *Contra Celsum* 3.73.

24. Hoffmann, *Celsus*, 54; Origen, *Contra Celsum* 1.9, 12. See also E. R. Dodds, *Pagan and Christian in an Age of Anxiety* (Cambridge: Cambridge University Press, 1965), 121.

25. Dudrey, "What the Writers Should Have Done Better," 61.

26. Hoffmann, *Celsus*, 61–62, 67–69; Origen, *Contra Celsum* 2.54, 59–75. Skeptics like Celsus reasoned, in the words of Vaganay: *"Qui donc avait vu de ses yeux le Christ au moment de sa resurrection? Personne."* ("Who then saw Christ with their own eyes at the moment of his resurrection? No one.")

27. Timothy P. Henderson, *The Gospel of Peter and Early Christian Apologetics: Rewriting the Story of Jesus' Death, Burial, and Resurrection* (WUNT 301; Tübingen: Mohr Siebeck, 2011), 213. The Gospel of Peter may well have been composed a decade or two before Celsus wrote. What the author of the Gospel of Peter attempted to answer were the kinds of objections and criticisms known in his time and then soon after were further developed by Celsus.

28. As Vaganay, *L'Évangile de Pierre*, 91, puts it: *Le pseudo-Pierre semble avoir eu conscience de ces objections possibles*. ("Pseudo-Peter seems to have been conscious of these possible objections.")

29. Tobias Nicklas, "Resurrection in the Gospels of Matthew and Peter: Some Developments," in W. Weren, H. van de Sandt, and J. Verheyden (eds.), *Life Beyond Death in Matthew's Gospel: Religious Metaphor or Bodily Reality?* (BTS 13; Leuven: Peeters, 2011), 27–41.

30. Henderson, *The Gospel of Peter and Early Christian Apologetics*, 213.

31. Hoffmann, *Celsus*, 16.

32. Adolf von Harnack, *Gegen die Christen* (Berlin: Georg Reimer, 1916). Since the appearance of Harnack's collection, a number of studies have appeared variously defending or attacking the German historian's conclusions. The scholarly opinion is divided over whether the pagan of Macarius' dialogue is Porphyry, a transcriber of Porphyry, or another. I accept Harnack's conclusion, i.e., that Marcarius was responding to Porphyry.

33. The charge of contradiction was commonplace, and Tatian's *Diatessaron* may have been intended to show that the four Gospels can in fact be harmonized. In any event, the apparent discrepancies and differences among the Gospels are in fact fewer and less severe in comparison to the writings of Greco-Roman historians during the period in question. See C. S. Keener, "*Otho*: A Targeted Comparison of Suetonius's Biography and Tacitus' *History*, with Implications for the Gospels' Historical Reliability," *Bulletin for Biblical Research* 21 (2011): 331–55.

34. R. Joseph Hoffmann, *Porphyry's Against the Christians: The Literary Remains* (Amherst NY: Prometheus Books, 1994), 32.

35. Hoffmann, *Porphyry's Against the Christians*, 34; John Granger Cook, *The Interpretation of the New Testament in Greco-Roman Paganism* (Studies and Texts in Antiquity and Christianity 3; Tübingen: Mohr Siebeck, 2000), 198.

36. Cook, *Greco-Roman Paganism*, 300.

37. As preserved in one of the Syriac fragments of Cyril's work against Julian. See Cook, *Greco-Roman Paganism*, 300.

38. See Vaganay, *L'Évangile de Pierre*, 91–92. Vaganay notes that the author of the gospel fragment took care to place the Jewish leaders close to the tomb, along with the Roman soldiers. In this way it would be impossible to challenge their testimony, for they saw everything clearly and discussed the matter among themselves.

39. One may well ask why a second-century Christian writer would embellish the gospel story in an effort to rebut contemporary critics. I doubt very much that the writer of the Gospel of Peter thought his embellishments were anything less than the truth. Stories and legends about Jesus began to emerge after the passing of the apostles and those they taught. The lines between "interpreted tradition" and unhistorical embellishment were not clearly drawn. Several apocryphal gospels and books of Acts appeared in the second and third centuries, characterized by the kind of embellishment we

find in the Gospel of Peter and the Acts of Pilate. Some of the embellishment was motivated by apologetic, but a lot of it is educational and devotional.

40. G. W. Bowersock, *Fiction as History: Nero to Julian* (Sather Classical Lectures 58; Berkeley: University of California Press, 1994). See chapter 5: "Resurrection" (99–119).

41. E. Koskenniemi, *Apollonios von Tyana in der neutestamentlichen Exegese: Forschungsbericht und Weiterführung in der Diskussion* (WUNT II/61; Tübingen: Mohr Siebeck, 1994).

42. See *Leucippe et Clitophon* 2.2.5, where the god of wine Dionysius points to the bubbling spring and declares, "This is the water of early harvest, this is blood of the cluster." On this passage, see Bowersock, *Fiction as History*, 126: ". . . the parallelism is hardly likely to be accidental. The language is far too close. . . ." Bowersock (*Fiction as History*, 134–36) also calls our attention to Petronius' *Satyricon*, in which the will (or testament) of the late Eumolpus requires his heirs to eat his body: "All those who come into money under my will [*in testamento meo*] . . . will receive what I have left them on one condition, that they cut up my body [*corpus meum*] in pieces and eat [*comederint*] it in the presence of the crowd . . . [you must] consume my body [*corpus consumant*]!" (*Satyricon* 141.2–4).

43. Bowersock, *Fiction as History*, 118. I follow Bowersock's translation.

44. It's gratifying to see my suggestion taken up and discussed, even if briefly, in Thomas J. Kraus, "EvPet 12,50–14,60: Leeres Grab und was dann? Kanonische Traditionen, *novelistic development* und romanhafte Züge," *Early Christianity* 5 (2013): 335–61, here 338 and n. 10.

From Oxford to Jerusalem—My Academic Journey

1. Jeremiah J. Johnston, *The Resurrection of Jesus in the Gospel of Peter* (New York and London: Bloomsbury T & T Clark, 2016), xviii, xix.

About the Author

Jeremiah J. Johnston, PhD, MA, MDiv, BA, is a New Testament scholar, pastor, author, nationally syndicated radio host, Bible teacher, and apologist, and he ministers internationally as president of Christian Thinkers Society. Jeremiah loves the local church and also serves as pastor of apologetics and cultural engagement at Prestonwood Baptist Church and dean of spiritual development at Prestonwood Christian Academy. Jeremiah's passion is working with churches and pastors in equipping Christians to give intellectually informed reasons for what they believe. Driven by the Great Commandment, Jeremiah's calling and the mission of Christian Thinkers Society is to equip Christians to love God with all their hearts and minds.

Jeremiah has distinguished himself speaking in churches of all denominations and has authored articles in both popular magazines and scholarly books, journals, and media programs. As a theologian who has the unique ability to connect with people of all ages, and as a culture expert, he has been interviewed numerous times, and has reviewed and contributed articles across a spectrum of national shows, including *Fox News, Publishers Weekly, CNN, CBS This Morning, Vanity*

Fair, *Premier Christianity* magazine and *Premier* radio, *RELEVANT* magazine, *DECISION* magazine, the *Christian Post*, the Moody Radio Network, and the Salem Radio Network.

As a New Testament scholar, Johnston has published with Oxford University Press, E. J. Brill, Bloomsbury T & T Clark, Macmillan, and Mohr Siebeck. He completed his doctoral residency in Oxford in collaboration with Oxford Centre for Missions Studies and received his PhD from Middlesex University (UK). He has also earned advanced degrees in theology from Acadia University and Midwestern Baptist Theological Seminary. Jeremiah is married to Audrey, and they are parents to five children—Lily Faith, Justin, and the triplets: Abel, Ryder, and Jaxson!

facebook.com/ChristianThinkersSociety
twitter.com/_jeremiahj
instagram.com/_jeremiahj
ChristianThinkers.com
Jeremiah@ChristianThinkers.com

More from
Jeremiah J. Johnston